Just Tell Me What I Want to Know About Wine

Just Tell Me What I Want to Know About Wine

Questions by
Dorothy Ivens
Answers by
William E. Massee

Publishers · **GROSSET & DUNLAP** · New York
A FILMWAYS COMPANY

The price of wine seems to vary unpredictably. Wine prices are affected by inflation, by supply and demand, by government positions regarding markups, and even by things as intangible as fashion and style. Prices listed are those prevailing in New York as the eighties began. You are bound to find wines in stores that will be more—or sometimes less—expensive than indicated here. This book is designed to help you judge all wines on a scale of relative values and thus can aid you in making knowledgeable selections now and in the future, regardless of economic fluctuations.

Contents

TELL ME MORE ABOUT WINE

Introduction

There are many marvelous wine books around these days, but they all tell me more than I want to know—at least to begin with.

I want some nice, easy answers to some "dumb" but practical questions. I want to know enough to be able to look after my wine needs as a hostess, a cook, a giver of gifts of wine on occasion, and a person who enjoys the magic of wine with food, no matter how simple the fare.

I am well aware of the delightful complexities of wine. I know from the size and variety of wine books around that a simple question like, "What is a good wine for fish?" (or beef or veal, etc.) is a very complex one for a wine expert to answer. To get me started, all I want is just a couple of suggestions from the infinite number of possibilities. *Then,* if my wine expert can give me, *someplace else in the book,* a list of alternatives for the wine suggested in each case (just in case my local wine shop is all out of it), I'll have just what I want to help me with my wine shopping, and I'll be learning something, too. Each purchase will be a step in the direction of learning about wine, not just a lucky or unlucky stab in the dark.

This is the way I felt when I sat down to write my questions. I made groups of questions on each category that I wanted to know about— Champagne, red wines, white wines, sweet wines, and so on. Then I presented my questions to William E. Massee, author of many books on wine, as well as a weekly column in the New York *Daily News.*

At first we had a problem. Mr. Massee knows so much about wine he had trouble not telling me more than I wanted to know. He kept giving me more information than I could handle in answer to my elementary questions. I think we finally worked it out, though, and I hope, after using his answers and following through with the back-of-the-book lists for a while, I will soon be ready to find my way in his and other fine wine books. In the meantime, I will be able to buy the wines I need with confidence and then enjoy them.

Dorothy Ivens
East Hampton, New York
& Bolsover, Ontario

Champagne

1 If price is no object, and I want just a perfectly marvelous Champagne, what are my choices?

Dom Pérignon or Roederer Cristal are the expensive favorites right now, about as good as you can get.

Traditional Champagnes, full and round in taste, like Krug and Bollinger and Charles Heidsieck, are always in the top class.

A particularly delicate Champagne, light in taste, is Taittinger Blanc de Blancs, and some people prefer it because they feel they can drink more of it. There is a list of great Champagnes in the back of the book (see page 95).

2 I see the term Brut *or* Extra Sec *often. What do they mean?*

Brut is the designation for the driest of Champagnes, and is the most popular type, so dry that it tastes best by itself or with hors d'oeuvre like salted almonds, ham, and caviar. Champagnes labeled Extra Dry or Extra Sec, still quite lacking in sweetness, are also delicious by themselves but taste better than Brut with more substantial food—and are often a dollar less per bottle.

3 Do I need to look for a specific year on the label?

No. Champagnes are usually blends of wines from different years. Each house tries to maintain a particular style from year to year. These nonvintage blends are called *cuvées,* a word that often appears on the label. They generally cost less than $12 a bottle for Extra Sec. Brut may be slightly higher.

When the wines of a particular vintage are considered exceptional, a firm may produce a Champagne from that year alone, putting the year on the bottle. These vintage Champagnes generally cost an extra dollar or so a bottle, but they rarely warrant the extra cost.

4 *If I want to serve Champagne before and during a dinner party, for six to eight people, and I want something prestigious but not too overwhelmingly expensive, what are my choices and how many bottles do I need?*

You'll need a bottle per couple, with an extra one or two for the exuberant. The famous houses long ago set standards so high that the least expensive from their lines can be your choice. Here they are:

Möet et Chandon White Star* Lanson Black Label
Pommery et Greno Extra Dry Perrier-Jouët Extra Dry
Mumm Extra Dry Roederer Brut
Veuve Clicquot White Label Bollinger Brut Special Cuvée
Heidsieck Monopole Taittinger Brut La Française
Piper-Heidsieck Extra Dry Pol Roger Dry Special
Charles Heidsieck Extra Dry Krug Brut

The most popular Champagne around the world is Möet et Chandon; the most popular in the United States is Mumm; and the most popular in New York is Piper-Heidsieck.

5 *For a small, rather formal occasion, such as a wedding reception, or for entertaining important guests, what are my choices and how much do I need for fifty people?*

a. When Champagne will be the only drink served and the food will be pâté, caviar, and very good cheeses?

---

*In this list and all other lists throughout the book, the first brand is not necessarily the best. In any list of wines, a wine may go up or down depending on vintage, luck, or skill.

b. For the same sort of occasion, only less formal, where other drinks will be offered as well as Champagne and the food will be a more substantial buffet? Could I use a less expensive Champagne?

For a party, the usual allowance is one bottle for four guests, considering that there are always some guests who don't drink. Two cases of a dozen bottles each should be enough for fifty people. To be on the safe side, a good liquor store will suggest an extra case, which you can return if unused.

a. The preceding list will assure you of getting fine wines. You might order half the wine extra dry and the other half *brut*—the last for those who follow fashion or are too excited to eat. Bear in mind that a couple of cases is a big order for most stores, so inquire about special prices. A 10-percent discount is customary when you buy by the case. Even with discounts, a case of Champagne can cost $150, which may be fine for a once-in-a-lifetime event. Still, it can be just as smart, and elegant, to serve Champagne first, then red or white wine with the food.

b. Champagne's worth all the attention you can pay to it; no wine brings a group together better for celebration, as corks pop and glasses of the bubbly are raised in toast—but it's extravagant. Champagne's wonders can be lost on a large party, particularly when food is being served to a hungry crowd. Something not so grand may be better.

One alternative to Champagne would be a sparkling wine, which every wine region makes. They are excellent and often taste better than Champagne with food because they are not quite so subtle and not quite so dry. Some that are around $8 a bottle are:

Asti Spumante	Piedmont, Italy, Often sweet.
Lachrima Christi	Campania, Italy. Often Sweet.
Vouvray or Saumur	Loire, France. Sometimes lightly sweet.

Saint Péray	Rhône, France. Quite dry.
Seyssel	Savoie, France. Very dry.
Rully	Burgundy, France. Dry and full.
Sekt	Germany. Often dry, usually ordinary.

. . . and American sparkling wines from New York or California.

Note: Be sure to ask for the sparkling—not still—versions of these wines.

Sparkling wines are called *vins mousseux,* "foaming wines," in France; *Sekt* in Germany; *Spumante* in Italy—designations that appear on the labels to identify the bubbly from the still versions. The word *Champagne* is reserved by international agreement for the sparkling wines of that region so named, a hundred miles east of Paris. The United States refuses to be a party to the agreement so that American sparkling wines can take advantage of the famous name.

Note: High prices for Champagnes have created a market for these sparkling wines, many of them tailored to American tastes. Seek out, particularly, Kriter from Burgundy and Ackerman-Laurance from the Loire; many good ones come in under private labels, notably those from the Savoie. Major Italian producers now produce good dry versions of Asti Spumante and Lachrima Christi. All of the best are white wines, some costing as much as $12 a bottle. Red sparkling Burgundy is a poor wine made for export, popular in England and the United States, a poor bargain at any price.

6 *Would you recommend Champagne punch for a small, formal party? And if so, which Champagne should I use?*

Champagne is almost too good for a punch, but the classic recipe is this:

Champagne Punch

juice of 1 orange
juice of 2 lemons
4 ounces Cognac
2 bottles Champagne, chilled
1 quart soda water

In a bowl pour the orange and lemon juice, add the Cognac and stir, then add the Champagne and soda water. You can add ice cubes, but the stylish way is to hollow out a block of ice and mix the punch in the hollow. (You'll need an ice pick and possibly a hatchet to chip out the hollow, but it's worth the effort.)

This batch will serve twelve people twice. The trick is to make fresh batches so that they will not be diluted by ice. The recipe can be doubled to serve a crowd of fifty, but you would have to start making another batch as soon as the first was set out—a much better practice than making the punch ahead. All ingredients can be cooled ahead of time. A batch of this punch can be made almost as quickly as you can squeeze the lemons and the orange.

Substitutes for Champagne are customary when serving a crowd. Any of the sparkling wines previously listed will make a good punch. Perhaps best would be the sparkling wine from the Savoie.

Some people like to sweeten the punch to taste with a couple of tablespoonfuls of sugar or a block of frozen raspberries or strawberries; others just throw in fresh berries for decoration.

You can also make the punch glass by glass: squeeze quarters of orange and lemon in a tall-stemmed glass, add an ounce of Cognac and a couple of ice cubes and fill with Champagne. Then top with a little soda water.

7 Do American sparkling wines measure up favorably to European?

Yes. We make some of the best sparkling wines on the market. Perhaps the best from California are made by Schramsberg Vineyards, and the best from New York State are from Gold Seal Vineyards. Several others are worth trying. You might buy a mixed case from the following list, enjoying the differences in style:

BRUT	EXTRA DRY	BULK PROCESS
Schramsberg	Hanns Kornell	The Christian Brothers
Domaine Chandon	Korbel	Weibel
Korbel	Weibel	Almadén
Hanns Kornell	Mirassou	Inglenook
Almadén		

Note: Bulk process refers to a method whereby the wines are fermented in vats, then bottled. The classic Champagne process involves fermentation in the bottle, which makes a more distinctive wine. Wines are also carbonated like soda pop, as in Lancer's from Portugal, but these are often poor, on a par with most German *Sekt.*

Sparkling wines made from native American vines have a special taste, wild and pleasing to some. Two of the best are from New York State, Widmer's and Great Western.

8 I want to give a bottle of Champagne to someone who, as far as I know, has no knowledge of wines. Which do you suggest?

You can always give the brand-name bottle from a major house, the one that's the least expensive of the line, for about $12. (See list in question # 4.)

Chances are that someone unfamiliar with Champagnes might prefer wines that are less dry, so Sparkling Vouvray or Asti Spumante might be best, along with a suggestion that they taste marvelous with fruit or pastry.

If the receiver is an adventurous sort, try one of the American sparkling wines (see page 7) unless, of course, he is of the belief that nothing good for glass or plate is made in America.

9 Which Champagne can I give to someone who knows wines and would appreciate a good Champagne with a lesser-known name, and one which might be less expensive than the obvious big-name ones?

Leading wine shops in every city have good but unknown brands they carry exclusively, and some of these are listed below.

Mercier	Gauthier
Ayala-Montebello-Duminy	Ruinart
De Castellane	Irroy
Charbaut	Philipponnat
Henriot	Delbeck
Laurent-Perrier	Deutz & Geldermann
Salon	Canard Duchêne

There are more than a hundred brands of Champagne recognized by the *Comité Interprofessionel du Vin de Champagne* and meeting their standards. Any of them are worth trying when you come across them. They'll be the real thing if they're from France, and they say Champagne on the label.

Shops with large volume, even celebrated restaurants, sometimes have private labels, Champagnes made especially for them, and these can be good value if they are two or three dollars less than the famous brands. These special *cuvées* are often made by famous houses, usually of interest to anybody who loves Champagne and adores a bargain. All wine buffs are interested in new wines that taste good, especially when the price is right.

10 *What is a good Champagne or sparkling wine, dry and pleasant, that I can buy by the case at no great cost, to have around for family celebrations and to give to close friends on small gala occasions?*

Sparkling wines from the Loire and Savoie regions of France are particularly dry and can cost as little as $8. Many sparkling wines from elsewhere are being made drier these days to conform to present fashion. Spain's Cordoniu is an example, drier now than it used to be. And, of course, American sparkling wines are good, too.

The sweeter the wine, the poorer the quality is apt to be. Flaws are hidden under sweetness. Be sure to ask if the sparkling wine you are buying is dry, getting assurance from store manager or restaurant steward when necessary.

11 *Which brands do you recommend when it comes to Cold Duck, Sparkling Burgundy, and sparkling red wines like Lambrusco?*

None.

12 *What's the proper Champagne glass?*

Any tulip-shaped stem glass that narrows at the top—and the bigger the better. The ideal shape is long and narrow, rather than bulbous, to concentrate the bubbles. If the bowl comes to a point at the bottom, then the bubbles will form a shimmering column as the bubbles rise—to tickle the nose.

Worst of all are the wedding-present kind, wide and shallow, that quickly dissipate the bubbles that took years to make. Such glasses, fine for sherbet, are said to be modelled from the breast of Helen of Troy, a myth that belittles the queen and does not help make the glass acceptable.

Only in a long and slender glass can you enjoy one of the real delights of Champagne—its appetizing aroma. There's a tantalizing smell of freshly baked cookies, according to some, golden fields of ripe grain, say others—indescribably Champagne, most people agree. The aroma is faintly of Cognac, for a good brandy is used to dissolve the sugar that is added to relieve the natural sharpness of the wine as it is made into Brut or Extra Sec.

13 *Are sparkling wines from California or the Savoie really good enough to serve?*

They are marvelous. And that's the trouble with lists. After a list of Champagnes that can number a hundred, of which only a score or so are marketed here, plus a list of special bottlings, plus a list of fine sparkling wines from Burgundy, the Loire and the Rhône, those of New York, California, and the Savoie may seem to rank way down. But they don't. They are excellent. They will please you. Compare any two of them and both will be good; they will simply be different. And that goes for all the lists in the book; buy any wine listed with great expectations.

Dry Red Wines

14 *What I really want to know is how to find drinkable wines at low prices to buy by the case. But shouldn't I taste a great wine first, to have a basis for comparison?*

Absolutely. Fine wines from the two greatest red-wine regions, Burgundy and Bordeaux, can astonish like any work of art. Taste any from the lists of the best in the back of the book on pages 96–124 to discover what all the excitement's about. Revelation can cost you $15 or less.

For your first taste of a great wine you may be most delighted by a Burgundy, ready to reveal its wonders when it's only five years old. More subtle Bordeaux reds may take ten years to develop, increasing in price, and with more time to run the risk of being damaged by bad handling or storage. My favorite Burgundy, typical and easy to find, is Volnay.

Volnay is the name of a township whose best wines are marketed under these vineyard names:

Caillerets	Chevret
Clos des Ducs	Clos des Chênes
Champans	Santenots
Fremiets	

There are more than a dozen highly regarded vineyards, but these are the ones you are most apt to find, rated as *Premier Cru*, or "First Growth"—the phrase to look for on the label. A wine labeled simply Volnay will be a blend from lesser vineyards, good but not great. (Volnay may be the best of all the Burgundy blends marketed under the name of a township, but such town wines are never in the same class as those with vineyard names.)

15 *If Burgundy and Bordeaux are the two greatest red wines, for my frame of reference, shouldn't I get to know the typical taste of each?*

Yes, and you might taste a typical Burgundy like the Volnay suggested previously, with a typical Bordeaux like Saint-Emilion. The best way to find out about wines is to taste one against another. These two would be good to taste with a leg of lamb.

Saint-Emilion is one of the four great red-wine districts of Bordeaux. The others are Médoc, Graves, and Pomerol. Although some of the greatest take ten years to develop, Saint-Emilions are often drinkable after five. Since they don't have to be stored for as long as others, with cost increasing yearly, many can be had for less than $10.

Vineyards are called châteaux in Bordeaux, because many of them were once part of grand estates. The vineyards are still called châteaux, to lend tone, even though there may not be a building at the vineyard. The best are listed in the back of the book, pages 115–124, district by district. Here is a selection from Saint-Emilion.

Château Beauséjour   Château La Gaffelière
Château Belair   Château Magdelaine
Château Canon   Château Pavie
Château Figeac   Château Trottevieille
Clos Fourtet

16 *What are some inexpensive wines to buy for everyday drinking and to have around for cooking?*

These are the wines that go to market with the name of a wine region or one of its districts. Shippers may market them with brand names.

Retailers can generally suggest good ones, but be wary of their tendency to recommend the most advertised or the most profitable. Here's a short list to choose from:

FRANCE	ITALY	ELSEWHERE
Côtes-du-Rhône	Valpolicella	Rioja (Spain)
Mâcon Rouge	Bardolino	Dão (Portugal)
Bordeaux Supérieur	Chianti	Zinfandel (California)*

There are so many good inexpensive wines that you really ought to buy a mixed case—for under $40—and see which you like. (You usually get about a 10 percent discount, twelve bottles for the price of eleven.) The wines should have an average cost of about $3; some fair ones are coming into the market from Romania and Algeria.

17 **What are some good inexpensive or medium-priced wines to buy in mixed cases, to have on hand for small, informal dinner parties?**

Your best bet is wine that is ready to drink within a year of the vintage, which means it will carry the previous year's date on the label, or at most the year before that. About 90 percent of the world's wines are meant to be drunk this way, within miles of where they're made. They are lively, quenching draughts—current wine or open wine, they're called—drawn from the keg and served in carafes. Only a few can keep their freshness long enough to be bottled and shipped to world markets. Winemakers everywhere are pressing grapes and

---

*California markets its best wines under grape names, of which *Zinfandel* is one, made in every district.

fermenting and filtering in new ways to increase the supply of these wines.

The model for all these fresh, young wines is Beaujolais, which comes from southern Burgundy and is the delight of France. Not wine just called Beaujolais, of course, for that is a blend of lesser wines from the district. Not even Beaujolais Supérieur, which is only slightly better. But the grade sold as Beaujolais-Villages, a blending from the better sites, is usually as pleasing as it should be.

Best of all are those bearing specific village names on the label, listed below. All of them taste best in the winter following the vintage . . . or in the spring . . . or in the following summer. . . . And only those from the villages of Morgon and Moulin-à-Vent continue to delight into the following year. Here is a list of good Beaujolais.

Brouilly	Saint-Amour
Côte de Brouilly	Chénas
Chiroubles	Morgon
Fleurie	Moulin-à-Vent
Juliénas	

Down in the Rhône Valley and over in the Loire and even up in Burgundy, winemakers are trying to capture the style of Beaujolais—with wines that are fresh and lively and light in alcohol (often less than 12 percent). Vinho Verde, from northern Portugal, and vineyards in northern Spain, around Barcelona, are following suit, and the idea is traveling east, into Italy, Yugoslavia, and Greece. Here are some to look for.

CÔTES-DU-RHÔNE	LOIRE	ITALY
Gigondas	Chinon	Bardolino Superiore
Cairanne	Bourgueil	Valpolicella Superiore

Wines from little-known Burgundy townships used to be patterned after their famous, more full-bodied neighbors, but now many of the vintners are fermenting quickly to keep the wines fresh and light. These are some township names to look for on a label.

Mercurey	Monthélie
Givry	Savigny
Santenay	Pernand-Vergelesses
Auxey-Duresses	Côte de Beaune-Villages

There are more complete lists on pages 97–114.

Many of these wines can cost $6 a bottle, even more. You will find, though, that many of the regional wines under $6 listed in answer 16 will be excellent to serve guests.

18 After serving Champagne at a small wedding reception for fifty people, what red wine could I serve with a substantial buffet, and how much should I buy?

You would need a couple of cases to be on the safe side, allowing three glasses of wine per person. The rule is that a bottle of wine provides eight 3-ounce servings.

After Champagne, you want a good young wine like those listed in answers to questions 15 and 16. But if you want to splurge a little, you might consider a Burgundy First Growth, identified on the label by the phrase, *Premier Cru*; these are listed in the back of the book on pages 99–114. Or you might consider a Bordeaux *Cru Classé* from the list in the back of the book, pages 116–124, preferably a Saint-Emilion.

19 What are some safe red wines to serve at dinner to someone who is very knowledgeable about wine?

You'll never go wrong if you buy the *Premiers Crus* (First Growths) of Burgundy and the *Crus Classés* of Bordeaux, phrases you'll see on the labels above or below the name of the wine. Lists of all these First Growths and Classed Growths are in the back of the book.

Don't forget American reds, which are discussed on pages 50–52.

20 *I want to take a bottle of wine as a present to a household where:*

a. Dinner will be simple, informal, and abundant—chili, pasta, or a barbecue.

b. Dinner will be formal or informal, but the host knows and cares about wine, and attention will be paid to the bottle I bring. What are some suitable choices?

a. My favorite is a jug wine or a magnum that costs about $5. Jug wines that cost less often lack character, blended to be bland and even lightly sweet to appeal to the widest possible market. The more expensive jug wines are often ignored, the consideration being that the extra dollar or so may not mean a better wine. But in truth, a jug over $6 may be an excess of production in a good year, or a type of wine a shipper has in abundance. A big bottle has a nice generosity about it, and the quality of the wine can be superior.

Here are some choices.

CALIFORNIA

Louis M. Martini Mountain Red
The Christian Brothers Claret
Villa Armando Vino Rustico

ITALY

Marino Castelli Romani

Note: Every region produces jug wines, like Calvet Club Claret and Ecu Royal from France and Juan Hernandez from Spain, but distribution is often limited. The wines vary widely, so the best suggestion is to try any that appear, hoping for the best.

b. Anyone fond of wine will know the famous wines, and the tendency is to buy one of them at an extravagant price—which you won't get to taste because the wine should rest for a couple of weeks before it is served. You can buy a young wine or a sturdy one that will stand the trip from the store—or a white or sparkling wine because they are not so complex as to be bothered much by the jiggling.

Wine buffs like less familiar or unusual wines—and would appreciate one that isn't too well known. Those listed below cost $8 or less, rarely more:

Rhône: Hermitage, Crozes-Hermitage, Côte Rotie, Gigondas
Loire: Chinon, Bourgueil, Saint Nicholas-de-Bourgueil
Spain: Rioja Reserva
Portugal: Dão, Colares
Switzerland: Dôle de Sion
Italy: Santa Maddalena, Lago di Caldaro
Hungary: Egri Bikavér

21 *Tell me about Italian wines. Are Chiantis all about the same quality? There are so many different names on Chiantis and they vary in price so much; is there a way to be sure of getting a good one?*

Prickly young Chianti in straw-covered *fiaschi* is a delight of Florence, but the best from more than two hundred square miles of vineyard in seven districts are mostly shipped in regular bottles. All have a neck label showing the *Marca Gallo,* a gold cock in a red circle, and one of the best districts, Rufina, is content with that. Other districts have their own symbols as well, and you might look for:

Chianti Classico, with a white cherub, or *putto*. Big wines.
Colli Fiorentini also uses a *putto*. Full wines.
Colline Pisane has a centaur. Light wines.
Montalbano shows towers. Fruity wines.

Less good districts show Romulus and Remus, a chimera, grapes. Chianti Classico is the best known, but many famous firms are in other districts.

Old Chiantis, called Riservas, must spend three years in wood, losing sprightliness and picking up a dry sharpness that is often harsh, but fine with hearty Italian foods. Styles vary from the major producers, and you might choose from the following, the Riservas costing perhaps $6, younger wines a dollar less:

Brolio Riserva, aged five years in wood.
Castello di Meleto, younger and less full, from Ricasoli.
Nipozzano, a long-lived, full, soft Chianti, from Frescobaldi.
Riserva Ducale, balanced and rounded, from Ruffino.
Stravecchio Melini, a classic Chianti from the house of Melini.
Machiavelli or Chianti Putto, typical and good for comparison, from Serristori.
Villa Antinori, considered balanced and distinguished, from Antinori.

There are more than sixty Chiantis on the market; some of the bottlings from small firms, at around $5 are excellent, and you might try any of the following:

Brolio	Pagni
Cantina del Papa	Suali
Nozzole	Verrazzano

The most renowned of Tuscany's wines is Brunello di Montalcino, like those above, to be tasted when you can find it. There are some 100,000 cases of the wine each year, and they supposedly last for fifty years but, like those above, seem best when perhaps ten years old. Some think they are too long in wood, but this is the Italian taste. They are particularly good with roasts and are marvelous with roasted chestnuts or with cheese at the end of a meal.

More than a hundred districts come under Italian control laws (indicated by DOC on the label, for *Denominazione di Origine Controllata*), but perhaps a dozen are produced in quantities enough to warrant consideration. The best are from the north—in the Piedmont, Lombardy, Verona, and Tuscany. Favorite young wines, at their best when three or four years old, are Valpolicella Superiore, Bardolino Superiore, and Chianti. There are dozens of others, including those from the noble French grapes, which are particularly worth trying.

22 *Are there some really good Italian wines? How do they compare in price to a comparable French wine?*

There are some marvelous and famous Italian wines, mostly from the Piedmont and the Valtellina of Lombardy. They are all made from the Nebbiolo grape, which is also called Spanna. These names are found on labels and are usually good buys at $5. The most famous wines use district names.

PIEDMONT	VALTELLINA
Barolo, full, big	Sassella, firm and full
Gattinara, full, fine	Inferno, big and famous
Barbaresco, elegant	Grumello, sturdy, long-lived

Italy now markets many wines with grape names; the noble vines of France, and some fine local varieties all warrant trying.

Nebbiolo or Spanna	Grignolino
Barbera	Dolcetto
Freisa	Merlot
San Gioveto or	Cabernet Franc
Sangiovese/Pinot Nero	Shiava

Winemaking, to say nothing of control laws, has improved greatly in the past generation, and those in the $4 or $5 price ranges are good to try when you're looking for robust wines. Italian wines generally resemble French wines from the Rhône—and are frequently lower in price.

23 *What Spanish wines should I know about besides Sherry and jug wines?*

The Spanish list worth knowing is short compared to the long list of Italian wines. The great region is Rioja, producing light wines that are some of the driest reds you can find. The best come from the Rio Alta district, but most are blends from the big companies. Good but often kept too long in wood, sometimes five years and longer, the old wines are used to give young wines the woody taste of age. The youngest, lightest wines are sold as *Clarete*, fuller reds as *Tinto*, the older wines as *Reserva*, even *Gran Reserva* and *Imperial*. Pink wines are called *Rosadas*. Wines simply called *Rioja* are good but lesser blends, selling for around $5. Leading shippers include:

Marqués de Riscal	Bodegas Bilbainas
Marqués de Murrieta	Bodegas Franco-Españolas
CUNE (*Compañia Vinicola del Norte de España*)	Federico Paternina

Good blended wines come from Valdepeñas, now a district in the vast vineyard region of La Mancha, south of Madrid. Lesser wines are now sold as *Manchego*, and most of the good jug wine comes from here.

Near Barcelona are the regions of Penedés and Alella, which produce some fruity reds but are known mostly for whites, particularly the sparkling wine of Codorniu, the driest of which is called *Non Plus Ultra,* now becoming popular.

Spain has more vineyards than any other European country and has begun enforcing a system of control laws, *Denominación de Origen.* Eventually, there will be as many wines to choose from as there are in Italy, but Rioja, Valdepeñas, and Penedés today provide most of the good wines available.

24 *Where do American red wines fit in the overall international picture?*

Americans have taken grapes from Europe, even developed some of their own, and now make wines that rank with the best anywhere. California joins Bordeaux, Burgundy, and the Rhineland as a great wine region. Grape names are used to identify the best wines.

Many small vineyards, rather preciously dubbed boutique vineyards, produce expensive wonders from Cabernet Sauvignon and Merlot, the Bordeaux grapes, that are fashionable to serve—and delicious to drink. Prices start above $6, and those most generally available are listed in the back of the book on pages 135–137.

My favorites, though, are those that cost around $5, or even less, and are produced in quantity. Look for the following grape names on labels:

UNDER $5	OVER $5
Zinfandel	Cabernet Sauvignon
Petite Sirah	Merlot
Barbera	Pinot Noir
Gamay Beaujolais	
Gamay Noir or Napa Gamay	
Carignane	

The Great Red Wines

25 I want to know more about the world's greatest wines. What's so great about them?

They taste marvelous. Just that.

A *good* wine can be delicious straight from the cask. *Great* wines stand out because of a perfect balance that takes time to develop, first in cask and then in bottle. They don't taste like much in cask, although experts can detect the potential in the bitterness of the tannin, in the fruitiness of the other acids, and in the floweriness of the alcohols that will eventually come together to make a single taste—a taste with balance. When such wines are drunk too soon, they taste rough or dull, because they are not yet composed. The very greatest wines take the longest to round out and to develop. This ability to develop is what is called greatness.

Tasting a great wine involves a lot of fussing that many people don't have the patience for. Common sense suggests you should taste maybe a hundred First Growths and highly rated wines before tasting the greatest. When you're ready to try one of them, here is the list of the greatest Burgundies and Bordeaux, the finest wines in the world.

BURGUNDY	BORDEAUX
Romanée-Conti	Château Lafite-Rothschild
Chambertin-Clos de Bèze	Château Latour
Le Chambertin	Château Margaux
La Tâche	Château Mouton-Rothschild
Richebourg	Château Haut-Brion
Romanée-Saint-Vivant	Château Pétrus
Musigny	Château Cheval Blanc
Bonnes Mares	Château Ausone
Grands Echézeaux	
Clos de Vougeot	
Corton-Clos du Roi	
Corton	

Note: There are a score more that could be added to each of these lists, all to be found directly after those above, in the back of the book, pages 97–124.

26 *You do not suggest I start out by tasting the very greatest of wines. Why are you reluctant to have me taste the best?*

You need a standard for comparison. The very greatest wines are so rare and famous that they are overpriced, but it's not that I'm trying to save you money. The wines are often drunk before they are ready—most take ten years to develop, many twenty—and they come on the market when they're four years old and cost $10 or so. Practically nobody waxing curious about wine has the patience to wait a decade or longer.

If you buy one properly old, a bottle can cost $30, but I am still not trying to save you money. You don't know how well the wine has been kept—very often it has been poorly cellared—and you may be disappointed. The wine should rest for perhaps a month after you get it home, at a temperature of 50°F., in a place free of vibration (and if you can't do this, drink lesser wines). It should be brought to room temperature (preferably no more than 68°F.) the day before it is to be served. It should be opened carefully and poured into large glasses. The glasses should be filled less than half-full, so the bouquet can be smelled properly.

You may have to wait an hour after the wine is poured before it begins to release its bouquet. You have to swirl the wine in the glass before sipping, so the bouquet will come out. You have to bounce it around in your mouth to get the full taste. (Some people "chew" the wine before swallowing, but it is better to suck in air, whistling in, which makes a sound many people consider vulgar and so refuse to do.)

A similar but lesser wine should be served before the *grande bouteille* as contrast. The food should not be sharp in taste, or spicy, because that may detract from the wine.

Great wines have subtle overtones not easily noted by those who have not drunk a lot of wines. Tasting them demands more attention than most people are willing to give.

Most pleasure for people not familiar with wine comes from those bottles ranked just below the very greatest.

27 What about vintages? Are they important?

They're important only for great wines from the great districts, just as vineyard names are important only to identify great wines. Regional wines and blends are meant to be drunk young, so a date on the bottle simply tells you that the wine is recent, but nothing about its excellence.

Great vintages are years in which a lot of great wines are made, along with many good ones. Plentiful vintages help keep prices down. Great vintages of the seventies with large crops are '76, '73, and '70. Great vintages with small crops are '75, '72, and '71. A big vintage was '74, but more good wines than great were made. (See listings in the back of the book, page 98.)

Older vintages to taste—if and when you get the chance—are '69, '66, and '61. There also were '59 and '52, '49 and '47 and '45, '37, and '34, '29, and '28—but most of these are long gone.

28 Do I have to memorize the vintages?

You might keep in mind the recent great vintages that produced a lot of wine, because quantity helps keep the price down. Plentiful recent vintages are 1976, 1973, and 1970. Big but not great was

1974. Small but good are 1979, 1975, 1972, and 1971; 1977 and 1978 are ordinary.

Vintages are important only for great wines of Burgundy, Bordeaux, and the Rhine. Elsewhere, they are mostly useful for indicating that a wine is properly young, of an age to drink, or not too old.

29 *Is the name all I need to know to buy a great wine?*

That's all. The names of all the great vineyards are on the official lists, protected by law. Called *appellation contrôlée* in France, that phrase will appear on the bottle, below the name of the vineyard. There are three things to look for:

1. The vineyard name (it should be on the official lists).
2. The phrase *Appellation Contrôlée* (which is a guarantee of authenticity for French wines).
3. The vintage (which tells you how old the wine is).

30 *Just how do you serve a bottle of great wine?*

I make quite sure I taste it at its best, which is easy, but requires some attention:

- The bottle should rest for a month or two after it arrives at the house, lying on its side in the dark, away from vibration. The wine needs time to settle. Bottled wines change with the seasons, so I make a point of drinking wines in midseason, preferably in the middle of winter.
- The day before serving, I stand the bottle up near where it is to be served, careful not to jiggle it in the moving.

- Just before serving the great wine, I open and pour a lesser but similar wine for the company to taste, for comparison.
- When about to serve the great wine, I pull the cork, careful not to jiggle the wine, pouring it at once in a second group of glasses. (A very old wine, ten years or older, may retain its wonders for only a few minutes, and if one waits too long, the wonders may be lost. Some old wines may take an hour or longer to develop after the cork is pulled, but I prefer to let the wine round out in the glass, rather than pulling the cork ahead of time; you may have to wait, but it is interesting to smell and taste the changes as the wine comes in contact with the air.) Because you may have to wait for the wine to reach its peak, I customarily pour it late in the meal, usually with the cheese course.
- When the company is primarily interested in the great wine, I sometimes serve it—and its lesser companion—by itself, before a meal, when expectation is high. Sometimes I serve it with a good cheese like Brie or a goat cheese, or a *pâté* and crusty bread. A great wine may not get the attention warranted when served during the conviviality of dinner.
- When I want to serve the great wine with the main course, I make sure the food will be simple—not too highly seasoned or strong in taste. Roasts are always good with great wines—ribs of beef, a leg or rack of lamb, veal or chicken. So is a marvelous steak.

Dry White Wines

31 *What's a nice, fresh white wine to serve as a before-dinner or anytime drink?*

Rhine wines are the classic choice, the only large group of light wines that are customarily drunk by themselves more often than they are drunk with meals. But every country drinks their own—before lunch and in the afternoon. Such wines are cool and quenching—a sip draws your attention when you're restless or want to relax—the tastes signal a change, a break, mild and pleasant, not shocking. They can be adjusted to your mood with a little soda and/or a slice of lemon.

The trouble is that Rhines are slightly sweet, or at least flowery, to many tastes. Such Rhine wines as Liebfraumilch, Moselblümchen and Zeller Schwarze Katz taste bland and vapid after a few bottles. Instead of going on to something better—the elegantly fruity Kabinetts, for instance—most people seek something drier.

Chardonnays are the fashion of the moment, the grape that produces all the great dry whites of Burgundy. Naturally, the most expensive are the most fashionable. Some cost $20 a bottle. There is extra cachet from drinking the fruitier California Chardonnays, many of them equally expensive. But many of them are too dry.

A good and simple wine—not too dry, not too sweet—reasonable in price is what's wanted. Several of the grapes grown in California produce ranges of such wines, as do various European districts. Here are lists, so you can switch from one to another.

AMERICAN	FRENCH	ITALIAN
Sauvignon Blanc	Blanc de Blancs	Frascati
Fumé Blanc	Sancerre	Orvieto
Chenin Blanc	Pouilly-Fumé	Verdicchio
Riesling or Gray Riesling	Saumur	Soave
	Vouvray	Pinot Grigio
	Muscadet	Verdiso
	Alsatian Sylvaner	Cortese

Winemaking all over the world has improved so much in the past decade or so that almost any bottle on the shelf costing over three dollars is a pleasure to drink. But bear in mind that cheaper wines may be sweetish, the sweetness added to hide flaws.

Blanc de Blancs, "white from whites," is a name borrowed from Champagne makers to identify regional blends that are usually quite dry. Buy wines by country or region, trying wines from different shippers or the various grades and grapes—to enjoy the differences, and to find wines you like. Variations are wide.

32 Aren't there some mixed drinks made with white wine?

Yes—the all-time favorite is the spritzer, which is classically made of Rhine wine with soda. *Spritz* means "fizz" or "bubbles" in German, and you can mix any proportion that suits: half and half, or mostly wine, mostly soda.

Burgundians use their lesser white wines—a Mâcon Blanc, or an Aligoté—with soda to make a hangover cure. They call it *rince cochon,* "rinsed pig," and it's like having a cold shower inside of you.

There's a liqueur made from currants in Dijon called Cassis, and you put a little in a glass—a tablespoonful—then fill it with white Burgundy. It is one of the most delicious drinks ever devised. It is called a Kyr in France, after a Dijon mayor who was much loved. There is a syrup called Cassis, but the liqueur makes a better drink. You can add soda to lighten it. Elegant restaurants use Champagne instead of Burgundy.

On the Riviera, there's a marvelous drink made by adding Champagne to orange juice, proportions to taste. It's called the Mimosa.

Add a little Cognac and soda to white wine and you have the beginnings of a punch. A punch is an English invention, the word meaning "five" in India, where it was created. "Something strong, something weak, something sour, something sweet" is added to a base; for instance, brandy, soda, lemon, and sugar are added to wine. Usually you don't need much sugar, but you do need ice.

Heated wine with brandy, a clove, and a slice of lemon, poured in a mug and stirred with a cinnamon stick is the classic hot toddy. You can use red wine or white, rum or another spirit instead of brandy.

Combinations are endless. You can use fruit brandies like Kirsch or Poire, all the citrus fruits or any berries, honey or maple syrup instead of sugar, any of the liqueurs. The trick is to let the taste of the wine dominate.

33 *Is it okay to put ice in white wine?*

Putting ice in a great wine ruins the balance that the maker struggled to achieve. It's like salting a dish before you taste it—not sacrilegious but not sensible, either. Put no ice in a Montrachet, a grand Sauternes, a Champagne. A three-dollar shipper's blend is something else entirely and may need ice.

Shippers make their regional blends with 12 percent alcohol or more to keep the wine from changing. That's about the strength of a weak highball, but it's a lot of alcohol for a wine; so much may make the wine taste heavy or strong. A wine at 11 percent or even less is light and easy to drink and an ice cube or two quickly dilutes a glass of wine to that strength. The ice mutes flavor, which is why brandy and fruit are added to a punch. A twist of lemon or a slice in a glass of iced wine is usually enough to bring up the taste again.

The matter is easy to judge. Taste a wine, then adjust it to suit—with ice, lemon, soda, even a little brandy. Chill the wine an hour or so on the bottom shelf of the refrigerator before tasting. Wines too cold lack flavor; often, a chilled wine needs to warm up to taste right and needs no ice.

34 How cold should a white wine be?

Not as cold as it is usually served. Cold mutes taste. An hour or so on the bottom shelf of the refrigerator is about right. Sticking a bottle in the ice compartment for half an hour chills the wine enough but shocks it, too. Slow chilling is best for fine wines, but three-dollar bottles are not hurt much, or at all, by quick chilling. An ice bucket, with water enough to float the ice, will nicely chill a wine in ten minutes. A few minutes in a cool brook is perfect. Overchilling need not be a problem. When a wine is too cold for you, let it warm in the glass.

Champagnes and sweet wines can stand more cold than table wines and may taste better very cold. When a wine is too warm, it's better to chill it some more and wait, rather than drinking it when it's not the way you like it. Salt added to the ice bucket cools the wine more rapidly.

35 White wines seem to vary in color from practically colorless to almost orange. Does the color mean anything?

White wines can have silvery or greenish glints in them, even golden tones, and pinkish tints when they're made from black grapes. But beware of wines that have tawny tones, like whiskey or tea—the brownish stain of rust. When air gets at wine, the wine can become oxidized, turning it brown—the color of old Sherry or Madeira. Such a wine will taste of straw, flat and brackish, as if cooked. The wine is said to be *maderized*; it will have the taste of Madeira, where it is desirable, but the taste is not pleasant in a white wine meant to be fresh, to taste of green things growing, of fruits or flowers.

A white wine turned brown is quite literally rusted. The wine has spoiled. Few dry white table wines can live five years without losing something. Great dry whites, and sweet ones, can live longer, ten years and more. Most white wines are best within two or three years of the vintage.

36 *What are some good, not-too-expensive white wines to buy in mixed cases to have around for small, informal dinner parties?*

Every region makes white wines, but a list of good dry ones readily available on the market is short. Those from eastern Europe—Austria, Hungary, Yugoslavia, Romania—are in the Rhine style, generally flowery; they are like those listed below from Alsace. Swiss wines are expensive; Greek wines have special tastes; Spanish wines tend to be bland; Portuguese wines are dry and good but hard to find, like those of the Savoie. Here is a list of generally dry wines, all of which should cost not much more than $4 or $5.

ALSACE
Sylvaner or Franken Riesling
Pinot Gris or Tokay d'Alsace
Pinot Blanc or Klevner
Traminer or Gewürztraminer
Chasselas or Gutedel
Müller-Thurgau
Riesling

LOIRE
Muscadet or Gros Plant
Savennières or Vouvray
Pouilly-Fumé or Pouilly-sur-Loire
Sancerre or Chavignol
Quincy or Reuilly

SWITZERLAND
Johannisberg (Sylvaner)
Fendant (Chasselas)
Neuchâtel
Aigle
Dézaley
Yvorne
Saint Saphorin

SAVOIE
Seyssel
Crépy

PORTUGAL	SPAIN	ITALY
Vinho Verde	Penedés	Lugarno
Dão	Alella	Terlano

37 *I understand white Burgundies are good and dependably dry. Could you give me a list of some to try, with a price range?*

Once you have found a store you can trust for wines under $4, you may want to experiment with a mixed case and a wider range of wines that may cost more. One of the most interesting of mixed cases is white Burgundy, all made from the Chardonnay grape, ranging from light Chablis to the full Cortons and Montrachets, in price from under $4 to over $20. Here are the less expensive names that Burgundian Chardonnays are called, a mixed case of them costing perhaps $50. (Many of those listed below can cost $6 a bottle and up.)

Mâcon Blanc
Mâcon Viré, Lugny or Clessé
Pinot-Chardonnay-Mâcon
Saint Véran
Beaujolais Blanc
Pouilly-Vinzelles or
   Pouilly-Loché

Pouilly Fuissé, overpriced
Montagny or Rully
Chassagne-Montrachet
Puligny-Montrachet
Meursault
Chablis*

Note: First Growths and Great Growths of the dry white Burgundies are listed in the back of the book, pages 109–111.

*Lesser wines sold as Petit Chablis are meant to be drunk in carafe, right after the vintage.

38 *Shellfish is so expensive that when I serve it I want to be sure the wine is right for it, even if I have to pay a little more. Could you tell me the names of some wines that go particularly well with shrimp, crabmeat, or lobster?*

Shellfish is generally bland and lightly sweet, so wines not too sharp in taste complement well. They need not be expensive and they should not be too distinctive. The best are fairly dry—even quite dry—lightly fruity or lightly flowery.

Muscadet from the Lower Loire is almost too dry, but is fashionable right now.

Flowery wines from the Middle Loire, like Anjou or Vouvray, are somewhat richer. They are made from the Chenin Blanc grape.

The Upper Loire produces fuller wines like Sancerre and Pouilly-Fumé, made from the Sauvignon Blanc grape, which also produces the full, soft white of Graves, the great Bordeaux district.

Fullest wines of all are produced from the Burgundy grape, the Chardonnay.

Try any two of them with seafood, particularly ones with those grape names from California. The wines are more flowery and fruitier there, splendid with seafood.

I like Rhine wines with seafood, those rated *Kabinett,* and if it's an Italian dish, I like an Italian wine like Soave.

There's no point narrowing the range. Any good white wine, from dry to half-dry, is good with seafood.

39 *What are some of the great white wines of the world?*

The only dry white wines considered great are those of Burgundy—Montrachets and Meursaults, Cortons and Chablis—and the best vineyards are listed on pages 109–111 in the back of the book, along with those rated good. To be great, a wine has to live a long time, developing with age, but dry whites are mostly ready to drink before they are five years old. Many good ones are drunk as soon as bottled, within a couple of years of the vintage. Only the sweet wines live a long time, and they taste best with fruit or a dessert.

40 *When I'm serving white wine before dinner—a jug wine, for instance—is it proper to serve the same wine with dinner?*

Certainly, when the wine goes with the food. People can take their glasses to the table. You can follow the jug wine with a different one if you wish. It's always nice, but not necessary, to serve a second wine—a better white wine or a red. The classic rule is to serve whites before reds, young wines before old wines, lesser wines before great bottles. But it's a matter of what gives you pleasure.

People like to taste a couple of wines at a meal. More than two can be confusing when people are also paying attention to the food and the conversation. That's why the classic rule is often broken and a particularly good wine is served when people first sit down at the table. Attention can wander away from the wine as the meal goes on, so there is nothing wrong with serving a lesser wine when the good bottle runs out. Whether you open another bottle of particularly good wine depends on the mood of the company.

Sweet White Wines

41 *I don't like sweet white wines, but are there some good ones I should know about?*

Tokay, Sauternes, and the Auslesen of the Rhine are the greatest naturally sweet white wines of the world—and all of them are out of fashion here. Tokay is so rare that it is expensive even in its Hungarian homeland; Auslesen are also rare—and they are also popular in the homeland—being priced accordingly. The sweet wines of Bordeaux, really from the twin districts of Sauternes and Barsac, are becoming fashionable for dessert in Europe, so their prices are rising. Few wines costing less than $10 can offer such delights.

Sauternes with pears and a soft cheese may be the finest dessert of all. A glass of Tokay with a ripe fig can be a definition of perfection. The sweet Rhine wines are usually drunk by themselves, offering tastes so compellingly luscious that drinkers are often speechless.

Note: Grapes are left long on the vine in California to get the noble rot whenever possible, and many good Late Harvest or "botrytized" wines are made. Most of them are sweet and rich, triumphs of winemaking, even when the market shows so little interest in sweet wines. They are invariably expensive.

TOKAY

Tokay is made by adding the juice from baskets of overripe grapes to the fermenting wine. The number of baskets, called *puttonyos,* determines the sweetness of the wine. This type of Tokay is called *Aszu,* and the more baskets the sweeter and more expensive the wine; three *puttonyos* is generally available, and five-*puttonyo* Tokay can be found.

The most intense of all is *Eszencia,* which is almost a cordial. One-hundred-year-old bottles occasionally appear. The wine can live forever. It was once reserved for royalty. The belief is still held that it is the greatest of restoratives and can make the old feel young again.

Tokay most readily available is the good *Szamorodni,* which can range from dry to sweet, and has a distinctive and appealing taste. The drier versions are a perfect afternoon drink.

Tokay is always shipped in small 50 centilitre bottles, which is a little more than a pint. It is made from the Furmint grape under government auspices and is shipped by a government export board.

SAUTERNES

Sauternes is made from grapes left on the vine, sometimes into December, where they are attacked by a mold that dries up the water in the grapes, thus concentrating their sugars. Pickers go through the vineyard several times, selecting only the moldiest bunches from the two sorts planted, the Sauvignon Blanc and the Sémillon. (Occasionally there is some Muscadelle for an extra trace of strawlike sweetness, but never more than 10 percent. The mold is called noble—*pourriture noble* in French, *Edelfäule* in Germany—and is *Botrytis cinerea,* which acts in damp, cool autumns to make wines of incredible ripeness and fruitiness. These sweet white wines can live for decades.)

Acknowledged to be greatest of all Sauternes is Château d'Yquem, but eleven others have been rated as *Premiers Crus,* and these First Growths are almost imperceptibly less glorious. They are listed in the back of the book, on page 124, but here are listed the incredibly good wines that are rated as *Deuxièmes Crus.* These Second Growths— often priced under $8 a bottle in good vintages—are among the best buys in the world of wines and are almost unknown.

SAUTERNES SECOND GROWTHS (*Deuxième Cru* on labels).

Château Filhot	Famous, drier than most
Château de Malle	Like Filhot, part of Yquem domain
Château Caillou	Popular, fine
Château d'Arche	Rich, lingering
Château Doisy-Daëne	Part of production is a fine dry white
Château Doisy-Dubroca	Distinguished, elegant
Château Doisy-Védrines	Plentiful, not well known
Château Myrat	Not château bottled at present
Château Broustet	Typical, rich
Château Lamothe	Known mostly in France; good
Château Suau	Known mostly in France; good
Château Romer	Good, known mostly in France
Château Nairac	American-owned, replanted

Key Words on the Label: Vineyards rated *Premier Cru* or *Deuxième Cru* will bear that phrase on the label, as well as the name of the château. There may be other châteaux not officially rated that can occasionally be found on the market, but these should be lower in price and may or may not be good buys.

Vintages: '76 and '75 are fabulous vintages for Sauternes and the wines will last through the eighties. The '71 and '70 are equally grand but should be drunk up during the eighties, as should two glorious earlier vintages, '67 and '62. All these wines can last into the new century, if well kept, but they might better be enjoyed in their golden years.

Prices: For best value, Sauternes should be bought as soon as the wine comes on the market, usually three years after the vintage; a high premium is paid for wines more than five years old. First Growths should cost well under $8 when first on the market; Second Growths around $6. Prices for Château d'Yquem start at around $12.

Sauternes is so famous that it is imitated around the world, and wines so-called should be ignored. Bordeaux shippers market blends of Sauternes, Haut Sauternes (which is supposed to be sweeter, but which is a meaningless phrase), and Barsac, but these are rarely worth the price when château-bottlings are available. American bottlers call their cheap sweet wines "Sauterne," but they are nothing like the real thing.

Sauternes can be drunk as soon as it is marketed, but Classed Growths in good years continue to develop during the first five years or so and can then stay at their prime for a decade and longer. They become more and more golden with age, losing their distinction only when they begin to turn brown.

Sauternes tastes best when iced, being able to stand chilling better than dry wines. Cold hides sweetness, so chilling for an hour in the bottom of a refrigerator is considered ideal. A wine too cold will warm quickly in the glass, and tasting the richness as it develops is a genuine pleasure.

42 *What could I serve Sauternes with?*

They make a fine dessert all by themselves. They are good with light pastries and with custards and other creamy sweets, like a dessert souffle. They are marvelous with fruit desserts that are not too tangy.

Maybe the sweet wines taste best of all with fresh fruits peeled at the table, particularly pears and peaches and apples, with soft cheeses. (Many people love very sharp cheeses like Roquefort with sweet wines.) Chocolate can conflict with the taste of sweet wines, but many people like the combination.

German Wines

43 Where do German wines fit into the picture of wines in general?

The Rhineland is one of the world's three great wine regions—Burgundy and Bordeaux being the others. The Rhineland is unique because

All its great wines are white.
The best are from a single grape, the Riesling.
They are not usually drunk with meals.
They range from flowery dry to lingering sweet.

The driest of them can be bought by finding a single word on labels—*Kabinett*. This may be the most surprising fact of all, because German wines have the most complicated labels of all.

Semisweet regionals like Liebfraumilch are the first Rhines most people taste. Some call them semidry. They appeal to those who claim not to like sour wines as well as those who say they don't like sweet wines, which is like describing a glass as half-full to somebody who thinks it is half-empty.

Marketed under a bewilderment of names, sweetish regionals are simple wines with little distinction, to drink instead of soda pop—with cold cuts, a hot dog, fried chicken. Frankenwein or Steinwein, and Moselblümchen are in the same class and can be found in most markets, but are not so numerous as Liebfraumilch, of which there are scores. Those costing under $4 are apt to be sweeter than $6 bottles. All of them are on a par with wines from a district, or *Bereich*, within a region.

These wines bearing a district name are lumped together and called "regional wines" by the trade. So are wines bearing names of a township or commune. The idea is to distinguish such blends from the wines of individual vineyards.

Here is a list of the most widely marketed regional wines and the district names by which they are sold.

REGION	DISTRICT
Mosel	Bereich Bernkastel
Rheingau	Bereich Johannisberg
Rheinhessen	Bereich Nierstein
	Bereich Bingen
Rheinpfalz	Bereich Mittelhardt Deutsche Weinstrasse

Once there were more than 25,000 vineyard names! Wine from a small plot would bear the name of the town and vineyard, such as Eitelsbacher Karthäuser Hofberger Kronenberg, famous as the wine with the longest name on the smallest label in Germany. In the seventies, it was decreed that vineyards had to be at least a dozen acres and those from the same slope or soil would have an overall name—*Grosslage*. A *Grosslage* might cross township lines and encompass dozens of tiny vineyards. The new law surely simplified things. Now there are only 2,500 names.

The best-known *Grosslagen* are little better than regional blends.

REGION	GROSSLAGE
Mosel	Zeller Schwarze Katz
	Krover Nacktarsch
	Bernkasteler Kurfürstlay or Badstube
	Piesporter Michelsberg
Rheingau	Johannisberger Erntebringer
Rheinhessen	Niersteiner Auflangen or Spiegelberg
Rheinpfalz	Ruppertsberger Hofstück

Shippers like the new *Grosslagen* because they can get substantial quantities of wines from the larger vineyards. Many of them are fine wines, but not vineyard wines in the old sense, where the least change of soil or exposure meant a different wine. An extended list of *Grosslagen* appears in the back of the book, pages 126–129.

The large vineyards of old remain as they were. A label bears the name of the town (with "er" on the end as in *New Yorker*) followed by the vineyard. There is the name of the grape from which the wine is made, the vintage, the producer, and the degree of sweetness.

Rhineland vineyards are the most northern, the same latitude as Labrador. Only on the best sites do grapes produce enough sugar to make wines of about 11 percent. Lesser wines have sugar added to the fermenting juice, the lowest grade being *Tafelwein,* a simple white table wine. Regional wines from the best districts are rated QbA, which means *Qualitätswein bestimmter Anbaugebiete*, or an approved wine with sugar added.

The best wines are not sugared, and bottles carry the phrase *Qualitätswein mit Prädikat*—"quality wine with a ranking." Look for this phrase on the label, in order to avoid sugared wine.

Here are the rankings from dry to sweet:

> *Kabinett* wines are dry, perhaps flowery.
> *Spätlese* means wine from late-picked, riper grapes. They are flowery, sometimes dry.
> *Auslese* means wine from selected overripe bunches. They are fruity, often sweet.
> *Beerenauslese* means wine from grapes in the selected bunches. They are rich and sweet.
> *Trockenbeerenauslese* means wine from shrivelled grapes. They are sweetest of all.

Basically, all you need to know to get fine, dry Rhine wines is *Kabinett*. These are the driest of the best wines, fragrant, springlike, a delight to drink. They are delicious with fish and seafood, with ham and other smoked meats, with all sorts of bread and cheese. They are most delightful, though, by themselves, lightly chilled, on a sunny afternoon.

The other ranked wines are sweeter. So many people have a prejudice against sweetness that the lingering wonder of a *Spätlese* or *Auslese* goes unnoticed. That they are marvelous by themselves, or with fruit and cheese, is lost—until you fall in love with the multitude of variations. Most people taste a regional wine like Liebfraumilch, decide it is too sweet and perhaps too ordinary—and never get around to tasting the drier, subtle *Kabinett* wines or those of late harvests.

Lightest of all are Moselles, the French word for the region of Mosel-Saar-Ruwer. The most famous are from the Mittle-Mosel, but the lightest are from the tributaries of the Saar and Ruwer and are wines not to be missed. The townships are rated in the back of the book, (pages 126–129), with their *Grosslagen.* (The *n* is added for the plural.)

The 500-plus vineyards are not listed, but if *Kabinett* appears on the label, you are pretty well assured of a fine wine.

The same assurance goes for the three other outstanding regions— the Rheingau, Rheinhessen, and Rheinpfalz. (They have individual sites of 100-plus, 400-plus and 300-plus, respectively.) A little-known area producing distinguished wines is the Nahe (300-plus vineyards), whose wines can be bargains. So can be those of Franconia, which has some 100 individual vineyards.

To get familiar with all these wines, your best choices may be *Kabinett* grade of *Grosslagen,* then progress to wines from specific vineyards and growers.

Dry Rhines are best two or three years after the vintage. *Spätlesen* lose freshness after five, but the *Auslesen* can continue for fifty years, gradually becoming as dark and pungent as old Sherries.

44 Aren't German wines always white?

Only the whites warrant exporting. There is a light red from the Blauer Portugieser grape of the Danube, fuller reds from Burgundy's Pinot Noir, called the Blauer Spätburgunder, to be drunk locally. Walporzheimers from the Ahr are drunk with smoked beef and ham, the local specialties. Local wines are to be tried every chance you get, but are never as good away from their homes.

45 How do I use German wines?

In the German way—in the afternoon or late in the evening. They are good with delicatessen, simple fish or seafood dishes—cold poached salmon, pan-fried trout, shrimp salad. Some people like to go up the scale of sweetness, nibbling cheese or eating fruit as they go. One of the world's best drinks is an ordinary wine with soda, half and half—the spritzer. German wines are unique, with a special appeal. There are those that prefer them above all others.

46 *Where do the best American wines come from?*

Mostly from small producers in California. That's where there are large plantings of European vines, *vinifera*, which make all the best wines.

Native grapes and their crosses dominate elsewhere, producing strange wines with insistent tastes. Drinkable wines come from New York, made from hybrids that are crosses between European *vinifera* varieties and native stocks. Hybrids and test plots of *vinifera* are grown in other eastern and midwestern states. Plantings are extending south, but production rarely satisfies local needs. Most of the wines you will get a chance to taste come from California.

Good California wines were not always so plentiful. Except for experimental plantings, most California wines made before midcentury were produced from ordinary grapes, or worse—Thompson Seedless, Alicante Bouschet, and others that gave vast yields of low-quality grapes. These standard producers, as the grapes were called, accounted for nine bottles out of ten—wines variously labeled burgundy, chianti, claret, rhine, and any other name of a European region or wine that might have sales appeal.

A small group of what came to be called premium producers— mostly in the Napa Valley—began marketing wines from *vinifera* grapes, using the names on the labels to identify the wines. The practice became widespread in the fifties, and the succeeding generation now uses the grape names for all the best wines.

47 *Are American wines as good as French wines and other great wines of Europe?*

Some are, particularly those from the noble grapes of the great regions. Super-vines have been developed, from individual buds, or clones, and then grown so that they are free of disease. Certified vines they are called, and they are now planted in all the best vineyards. There is great competition among the small wineries, whose best wines rate with Europe's best in tastings—and often cost as much, or even more.

Chardonnay, also called Pinot Chardonnay, is the grape that produces all the great dry whites of Burgundy, and the best whites in California. Try:

> under $6—the Christian Brothers Pinot Chardonnay
> over $6—Château Saint Jean Chardonnay

Sauvignon Blanc, the noble white grape of Bordeaux and the upper Loire, where it is called Blanc Fumé, produces fuller wines than in France, very dry or fruity and lightly sweet. Back labels usually indicate degree of dryness. Try:

> under $6—Wente Bros. Sauvignon Blanc
> over $6—Robert Mondavi Fumé Blanc

Johannisberg Riesling or White Riesling, the great grape of the Rhine and Moselle, produces generally fuller wines in California, ranging from fruity to late-harvest bottlings that can be quite sweet. Try:

> under $6—San Martin Vineyards Johannisberg Riesling
> over $6—Joseph Phelps Vineyards Johannisberg Riesling

Chenin Blanc, the great Loire Valley grape responsible for Vouvray and Saumur and Savennières, produces equally good fresh and elegant wines in California. Try:

> under $5—Mirassou Chenin Blanc
> over $5—Sterling Chenin Blanc

Cabernet Sauvignon, the great red-wine grape of Bordeaux, produces California's best red wines, on a par with most of Bordeaux Classed Growths. Try:

> under $6—Louis Martini Cabernet Sauvignon
> over $8—Heitz Cellars Cabernet Sauvignon

Zinfandel, a European *vinifera* of unknown origin, produces outstanding reds in California, on a par with the best Italian wines. Fresh and fruity when young, subtle and elegant as a great Bordeaux when more than five years old, many experts consider it the outstanding value in California reds. Try:

> under $5—Monterey Vineyard Zinfandel
> over $5—Pedroncelli Winery Zinfandel

Pinot Noir, which produces all the great red Burgundies, produces full but less distinguished wines in California, on a par perhaps with fair Burgundies, such as Santenays. Try:

> under $6—BV Beaumont Pinot Noir
> Louis Martini Pinot Noir

Petite Sirah, an ill-considered grape on the Rhône, produces full and fruity distinctive reds in California. Try:

> about $6—Concannon Vineyard Petite Sirah
> Parducci Wine Cellars Petite Sirah

Extensive lists of California wineries and grape varieties are listed in the back of the book, pages 132–135.

Rosé Wines

48 *Are rosé wines just a mixture of red and white wines?*

Grape color is in the skins—the juice is white—and the longer the fermenting juice is kept in contact with the skins, the darker the wine will be. The best rosés are made from black grapes (which are really purple or red) that have been separated from the skins before much color has been picked up.

The range from pink to inky is enormous. It is often hard to tell where red wines begin and pink wines end. Actually, they overlap, and while there is a prejudice against pink wines, it is based on a false notion that pink wines are pale and empty, without character.

The trade caters to the public opinion, offering sweetened inexpensive rosés with the claim that they can be served with anything. The sweetness makes them palatable enough by themselves, although not suited to most foods. Fashion is changing and many rosés are now dry, light, and fresh, meant to be drunk within two years of the vintage. The wines are as cheerful as they look, good with all manner of light foods, best when chilled, just the thing to serve when a red wine seems too much.

Rosés are made in every region from all the red-wine grapes. Most famous is Tavel, made from the Grenache. The best rosé of the Loire is made in the Anjou from the Cabernet Franc of Bordeaux; a lesser rosé with an orange cast is made from the Grolleau (Groslot) and is lightly sweet. Others are made from Pinot Noir, Gamay, Cabernet Sauvignon, and others—today's winemakers considering the low reputation of rosé as a challenge. Good dry rosés are listed below.

Tavel: neighboring Lirac is almost its peer, full and dry
Côtes de Provence: fruity when young, but quickly losing its freshness
Marsannay: Burgundy's light, fresh rosé of Pinot Noir
Anjou Rosé de Cabernet: drier and better than simple Anjou rosé
Rosato di Chiaretto: best is from Lake Garda

49 *When do you serve a rosé wine?*

The dry ones like those listed can take the place of any red, particularly those meant to be drunk young, like Beaujolais. Fresh and fruity chilled rosés are good with antipasto and all sorts of salads that are more than greenery, with smoked and spicy meats and egg dishes.

The lightly sweet pink ones—Portuguese rosé, Anjou rosé, most of those in jugs—are pleasant enough with dishes that have a sweet savor, but are perhaps best by themselves, well chilled, perhaps with soda and a twist of lemon, before meals.

Wines Before Meals and After

50 *Tell me what I should know about Sherry and Port and wines that seem like them—Madeira and Marsala.*

All of them are wines of the south, which vary wildly as they age. Brandy is added to keep them from changing. They are called fortified wines, ranging from 14 percent to 21 percent in alcohol, as distinguished from those called table or dinner wines, light wines that go to 14 percent and are served with meals.

Even the cheapest of Spanish Sherries, Portuguese Ports, Madeiras from Madeira, and Italian Marsalas are superior to imitations. Some of them can be had for $4 or $5 a bottle.

Dry versions, particularly Spanish Sherries, are traditionally drunk before meals, preferably chilled.

Sweet versions, particularly Portuguese Ports, are drunk after meals or with desserts and are not usually chilled.

51 *Aren't most of these fortified wines sweet?*

The range is wide. The greatest Spanish Sherries are dry; the greatest Ports are sweet.

Sherry is the most imitated wine in the world. True Spanish Sherry comes from a region south of Sevilla, around the town of Jerez, the name corrupted to Sherry by the English, who made it popular as the proper drink for morning and afternoon. Sweet Sherries are called Cream Sherries or Olorosos. The dry Sherries offer more choice. There are three dry types.

Dry: *Amontillado*—Duff, Gordon, Pedro, Domecq
Drier: *Fino*—San Patricio, Tio Pepe, La Ina
Driest: *Manzanilla*—La Gitana, La Guita

Port from Portugal is the only great sweet fortified red wine. Sweetness comes from stopping the fermentation with brandy before all the natural grape sugar has been converted to alcohol. Young wines are extremely fruity and are called Ruby, while older wines lose color and are called Tawny. These naturally sweet wines became an English tradition, the wines served after dinner, with walnuts, when the ladies had left the table so that the gentlemen could discuss matters considered of interest only to males. Vintage Ports that aged for decades were prized.

The name is borrowed for cheap, sweet red wines that are no match for those shipped from Oporto in northern Portugal, made from grapes grown in steep vineyards along the Douro River. More about Port in the back of the book, page 143.

Tawny Port is lighter in color and slightly drier than Ruby Port.

Sandeman and Dow are among the famous shipping firms.

Madeira, from the Portuguese island in the Atlantic, was the most popular wine in colonial America. Casks were sent on long voyages—there was always a special cask under the captain's chair—the constant rocking supposedly adding a special quality. Made like Sherry, Madeira has a certain cooked taste from being aged in hot rooms.

Madeira is generally sold as simply "dry" or "sweet." There is a range, however. The dry versions are called Sercial and Verdelho. A sweeter version is Boal (or Bual), the kind used mostly in cooking.

Sweetest is Malmsey, definitely for after dinner. One called Rainwater is a blend, paler and less intense in taste than the others.

Cossart Gordon, Leacock, and Sandeman are well-known brands.

Marsala is one of the best imitations of Sherry, developed in Sicily by an Englishman named Woodhouse to cash in on the Sherry trade. We use dry versions mainly for cooking. Italians drink sweet versions, some flavored with almonds or quinine. One of the least interesting has eggs added. Marsalas are usually sold simply as "dry" or "sweet." Florio and Stock are well-known brands.

All these wines get their character from the fact that they oxidize easily because they are low in acids. Air acting on the wines imparts a strawish, cooked taste and brownish color. Undesirable in a table wine, pleasantly compelling in these southern wines high in alcohol, the change is called maderization because the wines, with age, take on a taste and color like those from Madeira.

52 *Sometimes fortified wines, particularly Sherry and Port, say Dry or Cocktail on the label, but they turn out to be sweet and watery. How can I be sure of getting good ones?*

Security lies in buying the genuine article, not an imitation. Buy Sherry from Spain, Port from Portugal, Madeira from Madeira and Marsala from Sicily.

Spanish Sherries have yeasty, lingering tastes. When sales fell early in the century, imitators decided that less intense and lightly sweet wines would appeal. Dry and Cocktail "sherries" began to appear, along with similar wines called "port," "tokay," and "muscatel." To avoid the word *fortified* with its connotation of wine spiked merely to make it more intoxicating, California tried to establish drier versions as "appetizer wines" and sweet versions as "dessert wines." None of these wines were much more than alcoholic sugar waters with different colors. What happened was that all these imitations came to be known as the cheapest drink with the most alcohol, and, dubbed "Sneaky Pete," became the favorite of winos, thereby giving a bad name to the fine fortified wines still to be found.

For the range from dry to sweet in the good fortified wines, see the preceding question and answer. For more information about Sherry and Port, see the back of the book, page 143.

53 *Marsala and Madeira are called for in recipes, but can they also be drunk?*

The wines are certainly not fashionable, and are going the way of similar wines like Canary and Malaga and those made from the Muscat grape, like Malvasia. Marsala has an affinity for veal and chicken, the dry versions being used in cooking. Madeira is still considered the best of cooking wines for rich sauces, particularly the lightly sweet Boal (or Bual). All of these are drunk in their native lands and in England and northern Europe, but rarely elsewhere. Expensive versions are usually sweet and are excellent dessert wines. Inexpensive Madeira, like inexpensive dry Marsala, is excellent for cooking, while cheap imitations are not. Fino and Amontillado Sherries often replace them in recipes.

54 *Where does Vermouth fit in?*

Vermouth is an aromatic wine, which is a bland or neutral wine, fortified and flavored with herbs, barks, roots, and spices. Classed with Vermouth are name-brand aperitifs like Dubonnet.

Vermouth gets most of its flavor from wormwood flowers, *Artemesia absinthium*, which have a bitter taste of licorice. Vermouth was invented in Turin by a man named Carpano, but it became popular first in Germany, where it was named. (*Wermut* means "wormwood" in German.)

Artemesia absinthium is the plant whose leaves are used to make absinthe, now outlawed almost everywhere because of its extreme potency and alleged harmful effects to the nervous system. Similar licorice-tasting *spirits*, without wormwood, like Pernod and Suze and Pastis and Anisette, are drunk as aperitifs, with water and ice added, turning them cloudy.

Vermouth is both dry and sweet, based on white and red wines, each company having secret formulas of flavoring agents. The result is pasteurized to hold the taste. There is a special type of bitter Vermouth, the best known being Carpano's Punt e Mes. Italian Vermouth is traditionally sweet, French Vermouth is traditionally dry, although most companies make both types. Famous Italian brands are Cinzano and Martini & Rossi. Famous French brands are Chambéry and Noilly-Prat; an orange-flavored Vermouth is Lillet. Because neutral base wines are used, Vermouth can be made anywhere, the best-known American brand being Tribuno, now owned by Coca-Cola.

The tradition of flavored wines is ancient, any unpleasantness masked by sweetening. The Romans were said to be the first to use honey, and just about every herb and spice, root and bark has been used. Quinine was long a favorite, its bitterness offsetting sweetness, as in Dubonnet and St. Raphaël.

55 *Which of these wines is best for cooking?*

Madeira continues to be preferred in classic French cuisine, although certain dishes specify particular wines. Sherries are often used to replace the others. The only rule is to taste the wine before using it. If the wine isn't good enough to drink, it can spoil a dish.

56 *If a bottle isn't finished at one sitting, can the rest be kept for another day or longer? In other words, what does one do with leftover wine?*

An opened bottle, recorked, will keep for three or four days in the refrigerator but will gradually lose freshness. (If the leftover wine is put into a smaller bottle so that there is no air space above the wine, it will keep as well as if it had never been opened. Most people prefer to drink leftover wines within a day or two.)

Leftover wines are marvelous for cooking, even when they have soured. (They can also substitute for vinegar.) However, if the smell or taste of an old wine is unpleasant—musty or rank or foul with a smell like wilted vegetables—the wine is best discarded.

57 *How can wine be stored in a city apartment?*

Wines are sturdy and will stay in good condition for a season or two on a shelf or in a closet. Light, vibration, and varying temperature are the elements that cause a wine to fall apart and age fast. A rise in temperature much beyond 70°F., or daily variation of ten degrees can blunt a wine in a month or so; vibration from an elevator or subway can wreck a wine in weeks; the stamp of feet or the slam of doors takes longer. Sunlight can spoil a wine in days.

Corrugated whiskey cartons laid on their sides offer some insulation; they can be stacked two or three cases high. Space near the floor is coolest and wines keep better in low cabinets rather than on high shelves.

Ideal storage temperature is under 55°F., but temperatures in the low sixties will allow wines to hold together for a couple of years. At the higher temperatures, they will age more quickly. Reds that will be kept for more than five years should be stored in ideal temperatures.

58 *What is a good wine to have with Chinese food?*

White wines not too dry generally taste best. One favorite is Graves Supérieur from Bordeaux. (Sichel & Fils bottles one called Wan Fu, the wine of a thousand happinesses, expressly for the purpose.) A Chenin Blanc or Sémillon from California can taste good. And there is always rosé, preferably one that is not too sweet.

59 *Is it necessary to serve different wines in different glasses?*

Any glass will do, just so long as it is big enough—say 9 to 11 ounces—preferably of clear glass so that you can see the wine. Normal fill is about one-third, and certainly less than half, so that the wine can be swirled in the glass. The swirling lets air at the wine, causing a little of the alcohol to evaporate and release the aromatic qualities of the wine. The best glasses narrow at the top, serving to capture the aromas so that they can be smelled readily. The empty space in the glass above the wine can be thought of as a kind of chimney.

Wine glasses generally are stemmed so the glass can be held by the stem and the wine can be looked at. Good wines have a marvelous clarity and a splendid range of colors—meant to be enjoyed. There is special stemware for all the great wines—a tulip shape for Bordeaux, a rounder apple shape for Burgundy, a smaller peach shape with an especially long stem for Rhines; but what is needed is simply a large, clear glass that narrows at the top.

Such an all-purpose glass can be used for all wines, even Champagne, Sherry, and Port. In our house we use such a glass for mixed drinks, as well—and for brandies.

It is customary to have separate glasses for each wine served—there is the pleasure of anticipation on seeing a range of glasses at each place setting—and these can be the same all-purpose ones. Special glasses, when you have them, give an indication of the wines to be served; when glasses are all the same, mystery remains until the wine is poured. There can be confusion when similar wines are served in the same-size glasses, but this is part of the fun.

Purists like a clear glass, unadorned, the better to see the wine. Wines seem to taste best from glasses with thin rims, rather than those with a thick rim (called a safe edge) which is supposed to make the glass less easily breakable, but doesn't. Cut glass and tinted glass may obscure the wine, but they are often works of art and look splendid on a table. The only really bad glass is the shallow, wide-mouthed Champagne *coupe* so popular as a wedding present; it sloshes easily and dissipates the laboriously produced bubbles and is better used for sherbets and fruit cocktails.

Straight-sided glasses without stems are fine for jug wines and those that don't deserve special attention. They can be filled to the brim —as they are in Paris bistros and where wine is poured straight from the cask; but the glass should be clear, so that you can see what you're drinking.

60 When wine is served with a meal, is water served, too?

Suit yourself. It's customary here, not in Europe. Water tastes delicious after a meal where wines are served but is distracting with the meal.

61 How many wines are served at the traditional wine dinner?

Wines used to be customary with every course—Sherry with the soup, white wines with the fish, reds with the roast and the cheese, sweet wines with dessert, and Port to follow. Champagne was served before dinner, Brandy with the coffee. Five-course meals are still served for occasions. Wine dinners might include two whites and two reds—but are rarely the bountiful affairs of yesterday's *haute monde*. Two or three wines at a convivial dinner are most pleasing today.

62 *Are grapes ever crushed by feet anymore?*

The bare human foot is still the best possible instrument for crushing grapes without smashing the pips or stems, both of which contain harsh elements that put off-tastes in the wine. This sanitary age considers feet, even well washed, improper or maybe even dangerous to health, an attitude that ignores the fact that fermentation is a sterilizing process.

Countrymen still trample the grapes from farm vineyards in remote parts of Europe; men wearing boots crush the grapes in the Sherry vineyards around Jerez, and the grapes for Porto are still sometimes trodden by men who chant songs to the lilt of an accordion.

The trouble with treading grapes is that the process is slow, allowing air to get at the grapes. Modern pressing machines do the job quickly and well, with a minimum of air getting at the wine. But that loses the romance and frolic. Some people, obviously sentimentalists, think wines lost something when treading disappeared.

63 *Are there any basic rules for cooking with wine?*

Most basic is to cook only with wines you are willing to drink. A poor wine can ruin a dish.

What is sold as "cooking wine" is the most ordinary wine (usually from a second pressing of the grapes and commonly imported from

Spain) that has salt added to it so that it cannot be drunk, a hangover from Prohibition days.

The taste of the wine adds flavor to a dish, helping to blend and bring out tastes. Recipes are devised so that the taste of wine is not overpowering but a complement to other flavors; using too much is far worse than not using enough.

The alcohol cooks away after only a couple of minutes of cooking; even added at the last minute to a hot dish, the alcohol will boil off—leaving only its taste.

The best wines for cooking are good sound wines, preferably young ones. The subtleties of great wines are lost in a dish, disappearing in the cooking process. To use a great wine in cooking is a waste and a pretension.

Leftover wine that has lost its attractiveness for drinking can be excellent for cooking because only the basic constituents contribute to the dish. Even a wine that has turned to vinegar can be used, its acids serving as a tenderizer. Wines so far off in taste as to be unpleasant, though, can add unpleasant flavors to a dish.

The fruit acids in a wine are more subtle as a tenderizing agent than strong vinegars, so wines are particularly good as a base for a marinade.

Red and white table wines add subtle overtones to a dish. Fortified wines like Sherry and Port, flavored wines like Vermouth, have strong tastes and are used in small amounts. When substituting Vermouth for white wine in a dish, the general rule is to use half as much as you would of table wine, or cut half-and-half with water.

Wines like Madeira and Marsala are usually used to finish a dish, rather than during cooking.

64 *Can children have dishes cooked with wine?*

The amount of wine used in a dish rarely exceeds a cup or two, but even if there were much more, there is no need for concern. Alcohol boils off in the first few minutes of cooking, even disappearing when stirred into a hot dish.

65 *Should a person on a slimming diet avoid wine?*

To the contrary—wine can be a most desirable part of a diet. Dry wines contain no sugar, and these are the ones that most enhance the taste of food, averaging about 12 percent alcohol. (This is equal to 24 proof, roughly that number of calories per ounce.) The generally bland food on a diet is made tolerable by the sharp and pleasing taste of wine. A normal serving of 3 ounces of table wine is about 75 calories, just the thing to make mundane cottage cheese or tuna fish taste edible.

Wines have been known for centuries to aid digestion, perhaps mostly because the fruit acids help break down various foods, and other benefits have been claimed for the vitamins and minerals and trace elements in wine. These scarcely matter. Wines taste good and have that endearing ability to cheer the drinker. Health benefits aside, a dieter would be wise to include wine in the regime, if only for the fun of it—to make up for his deprivation.

66 *What is the best kind of corkscrew?*

One that has its coil, or worm, made of round wire, rather than a spiral with a cutting edge. Most cheap corkscrews have cutting edges that tend to chew up a cork. The point of the coil should be in line with the spiral, not the center, so that the wire can follow the point into the cork. (Because the point is offset, it should be inserted slightly off center.) The corkscrew, not the bottle, is twisted as the cork is pulled, so that the wine won't be jiggled. Some corks stick to the neck of the bottle, so corkscrews with levers or double screws exert more force and make the cork easier to pull than do corkscrews that have only fingerholds.

67 *Why are wines so expensive in restaurants?*

The best restaurants charge twice cost, on the idea that handling and serving warrant a return. A bottle costing $4 would cost $6 in a retail store where the average markup is usually 50 percent, so $8 can be considered a reasonable restaurant price. (Some consider this not reasonable when the cost is $10 and the wine is sold for $20.)

Many restaurants charge three and four times cost because they can get away with it. People don't like to complain, even when they should. Until they do, restaurants will continue to charge high prices, figuring that people on expense accounts don't care and others don't know enough to be aware that they are being overcharged.

68 *How do you choose wine from a restaurant wine list?*

Check first for good values:

A nonvintage Champagne from a good house should cost around $15.

A Côtes-du-Rhône should cost about $8.

California Cabernet from a good firm noted for reasonable prices, like Louis Martini, Wente Bros., or The Christian Brothers, should cost $10 or less.

Chianti, Valpolicella, or Bardolino from a well-known shipper should cost $6 or $10.

The trick is to find a wine on the list that you know. If it is reasonably priced, this is a good sign, although wine lists are notoriously inconsistent.

Many restaurants offer wine by the glass or carafe. Ask what the wine is, and if the selection is from a good house, this may be the best buy.

A rule of thumb is to pay no more for the wine than twice the cost of the dish it is to be served with.

Avoid *all* the high-priced wines on the list. You don't know how they have been kept.

Seek out the least expensive wines on the list. If they are good wines, try them. If you are not familiar with them, or if they are poor selections, you might better buy beer.

Ask the owner or the wine steward what he would suggest. If the choices—he should make at least two—are in the middle price brackets, the suggestions are worth following because he knows his cellar better than you do. Wines featured by restaurants may be good wines because they are usually bought at a discount in large lots.

Scarce wines, like the famous Burgundies and Bordeaux châteaux, will always be high in price. They are only bargains if the restaurant bought the wines as soon as they came on the market and took the trouble to store them until they were ready to drink. Although some restaurants automatically add 10 percent each year to the price they paid for a wine, many can't be bothered with the bookkeeping and continue selling the wine at twice what it cost.

Some people like to look at the wine list first. An appealing wine may suggest what to choose from the menu.

There is no excuse today for a good restaurant not to have a good selection of wines at sensible prices. A restaurant without good wines to choose from is just another clip joint.

69 *Should wine be served from one of those wine baskets?*

They are considered to be pretentious, more a sign of ignorance than sophistication. But this attitude is somewhat snobbish because a basket or cradle is more steady on the table than a bottle alone. A bottle need not be tipped up and down so much when it is poured from a basket, which is certainly an advantage with an old wine that may contain some sediment. Baskets make life simpler for the restaurant, reducing the danger of spilling, an advantage not undesirable in the sometimes frantic serving of a dinner at home.

70 *When is decanting a wine necessary?*

Hardly ever, because wines are filtered so much to keep them clear that they rarely throw a sediment. This is a shame, because heavy filtering takes the guts out of the wine. Motelike specks in a wine, even tartrate crystals that form on the bottom of the cork, do not hurt a wine a bit.

Wines made in the old-fashioned way may show a deposit in the bottom when the bottle is held up to a light. Such wines are usually decanted—poured into a clear pitcher or decanter in a steady stream until the sediment begins to flow into the neck of the bottle. Usually an inch or so of wine remains with the sediment after the pouring, and this is thrown away.

 71 *Wine talk often sounds ridiculous, with phrases like "a pretentious little wine," words like* body, balance, elegance. *Do such words and phrases really mean something, or are they as silly as they sound?*

Lots of wine talk is boring and pompous because we have few precise words for taste, not many beyond the basic ones of *bitter* and *sweet, sour* and *salty.* So we describe wines in terms of pictures that the tastes remind us of: wines are like women or songs, with textures like cloth, colors like gems. Tastes are hard to put into words; smells are even more difficult.

An expert's wine language is shorthand, a professional jargon, complexities summed up in a word. Much of it is French, as is the language of love and diplomacy, and sometimes less than clear when a word with a common meaning is given a special one. Many sound precious, although an expert is expressing something down-to-earth and sensible in the true meaning of the word. The following are some examples:

Acidity is the amount of fruit acids in a wine that, like lemonade, can be puckery or merely add a taste of freshness to the wine and a feeling of liveliness in the mouth. The various malic, tartaric, and citric acids, without which the wine would be bland and insipid, give a taste to the wine best described as tart. Tannin imparts a bitter taste to the wine—this lessens as the wine ages—a quality often referred to as astringent. The word *sour*—which is the vinegar taste of acetic acid—is avoided, every effort being made to keep this out of the wine.

For the academic, *volatile acidity* is the acetic acid of a wine, kept at a minimum because of unpleasant taste and smell. *Fixed acidity* is the sum of all the fruit acids in a wine, essential to flavor. *Total acidity* is the sum of these two. *Real acidity* is commonly used to refer to intensity of the acid taste, what a winemaker calls the pH of a wine, represented as a number. A wine with a pH of less than 3 would be tart, a pH of nearly 4 would be neutral and bland—and uninteresting.

Balance is that quality of a wine, where no element is so pronounced as to detract from the taste. One can speak of the acidtannin balance, where the fruity acids are in harmony with the bitter taste of tannic acid, or of the alcohol-acid balance, where the flowery qualities of one and the fruity qualities of the other are in harmony. A light wine can have a balance described as elegant, while a full wine can have more pronounced tastes in equilibrium. Balance is a most desirable characteristic.

Body describes the wateriness of a wine, one light in body, tasting watery, but not so much so that the taste is unsatisfactory. Some wines, light Moselles, for instance, have been described as glorious water. A full-bodied wine like a Rhône, may have so much substance that one can almost chew it, a quality the French call *maché*. The quality of this fullness can be *velvety* or *silky*, giving a sense of texture in the mouth, and Rabelais referred to Vouvray as a wine with the texture of taffeta. There is a certain amount of glycerine naturally in wine, particularly reds, that contributes to the feel in the mouth, a quality commonly called smoothness, a word too imprecise for the winemaker.

Bouquet is the collection of smells in a wine, flowery alcohols and fruity acids, that form a unity when the wine is good. *Perfume* refers to the fragrances and aromas, usually light and of the grape, found in a young wine right after fermentation. These develop into the bouquet.

Corky describes a wine that smells and tastes of the cork, not of the wine. The French say the wine is *bouchonné*. The odor is a sign that the cork has rotted and the wine has been spoiled. When the taint is slight, there is always the hope that swirling the wine in the glass will cause the air to dissipate the unpleasantness, but this is not so. A good wine steward will sniff the cork after he has pulled it to verify that the wine is sound and smells of the wine, or he will present the cork to the host for verification. (The host is traditionally responsible for seeing that the wine is good and can be poured.)

A corky bottle is never served and is replaced with another bottle. (The cork can be returned to a store for replacement, and a good store will accept the cork with no questions asked.) Corks of good quality can last for twenty years, after which the bottle is recorked, a fact that should be noted on the label.

Corkiness is rare—noticeable in one bottle out of a hundred, perhaps—and usually occurs because a bottle is left standing so that the cork dries and shrinks. (This is why bottles are stored on their sides, to keep the cork wet.) A good winemaker uses long corks, branded with the name of the vineyard from which the wine comes, the producer, and the vintage.

A long cork, over two inches, is used for wines that are meant to stay long in the bottle. Short corks and screw tops are used for wines meant to be drunk within a year or so of bottling.

Dry—the French is *sec*—means the opposite of *sweet*. *Sour* won't do, for a sour wine is one that has spoiled. (*Vin aigre* is French for "sour wine," vinegar.) *Dry* as the opposite of *sweet* is hardly the perfect word for something wet, but is used for want of something better.

Elegance is used to describe a harmony of smell and taste, not common or ordinary. (See *Finesse*.) The word may bring up a picture of someone in a tailored suit, rather than one off the racks, or perhaps a glass of crystal without etching or engraving. You will know an elegant wine when you taste it—and you might better find your own words, natural to you, rather than the professional term. You can have fun making up wine words, which is better than using professional terms loosely.

Finesse is a word that describes wines without coarseness, displaying breed or distinction—a balance of elegant qualities. It is a characteristic of a fine wine.

Finish is a tasting term popular with the English and refers to the taste left in the mouth after the wine has been swallowed. The wine should not seem to fall away or leave a taste of sharpness or bitterness in the mouth. The aftertaste should be a continuation of the taste, gradually diminishing.

Good wines ("*bons vins*" in French) is the term used by the trade to mean wines that aren't bad, that have nothing outstanding wrong with them. A taster means something a little more positive when he says a wine is good, meaning that all qualities are in balance and representative of the region and grape it is made from; it is high praise.

Great wines ("*grands vins*" in French) is the term used by the trade to mean wines that have a reputation. The taster uses the term to refer to a wine that improves with age, is consistent from year to year, and characteristic of the grape and vineyard from which it comes. The smell of the wine, its first taste, the middle taste, and the after-taste form a unity, a variation on a theme—no less than a wonder.

Note: There are various off-tastes noticeable in wines. A wine tasting too strongly of oak is called *woody;* one tasting of stems is called *stemmy,* green and harsh, and this is related to a *steely* taste, which is unpleasantly metallic. Various chemical smells—of sulphur, which is used as a preservative, particularly—that remind one of a medicine chest or school laboratory, should not be in a wine, nor should rank vegetable or rotten fruit tastes.

There should be nothing unpleasant in the wine, no taste of cellar or earth or mold. The smell and taste is so complex that bad tastes stand out, like a tin can in the woods. A light smell of wood or earth, reminiscent of new wood or mossy ground, is not unpleasing, and these ephemeral odors and tastes instantly stir memories—all of which should be pleasing. Wines often remind people of berries and fruits, flowers and spices—wines are said to taste of raspberries or currants, of apples or violets or cinnamon—and these words are frequently used to describe wines.

CHECK LIST A student friend insists that a list of wine words, whether professional or casual, would be helpful to make judgments about wines. You could use a list to check off the various qualities indicated by the words. Good and negative adjectives are listed below, to help you rate the wines when you want to decide that a wine is good, bad, or indifferent.

GOOD QUALITIES	POOR QUALITIES
Brilliant	Hazy
Clear	Cloudy
Clean	Off, flawed
Delicate	Heavy, rough
Distinguished	Common
Fine	Dull
Fragrant	Odorless
Fresh	Flat
Full	Thin
Noble	Ordinary, common
Ripe, developed	Green, too young
Rounded	Unbalanced
Sound	Sick, unpleasant
Sturdy	Weak, vapid
Tart, lively	Sour, vinegary

72 How do you feel about serving cocktails and hard liquor before a dinner with wine?

If you allow an hour for drinks before dinner, nobody is apt to drink too much and spoil their enjoyment of the wine.

When one or two fabulous wines are being served, and you want people to pay attention to them, a Scotch and soda or dry Sherry are the best drinks, better than too sweet or too potent cocktails. You could also just serve Champagne, or wine drinks, but let your guests know it is going to be that kind of party, with wine as the focus.

73 *When a dinner guest brings a bottle of wine as a gift, should I serve it at this time or put it away for another occasion?*

When house presents were a box of candy or flowers they were usually set out—if you could find a bowl or a vase. Champagnes and white wines—and Sherries and Ports—can be served in the same tradition when they suit the dinner. So can young red wines and rosé wines. When the wines don't suit, the best you can do is say so and serve it at another meal.

When the red wine is a grand bottle—that usually means a bottle costing five dollars or more—it's usually shook up from the handling. Just the jiggling bringing it from the neighborhood store upsets the wine. The bottle should rest for a week, at least, and a month is better, so it will taste at its best.

The bringer of the bottle may not know that, so you have to judge whether the intention is that it should be served. If so, there is no choice—unless you can exclaim that the wine is so good it needs resting for a time. This sounds like an excuse, so you might beg off by thanking the giver and say you look forward to serving it the next time the giver is a guest.

74 *Lots of wines have names hard to pronounce and I hate to make a fool of myself by saying them all wrong. Why haven't you put phonetic spellings all through the book?*

Nobody agrees on phonetic spellings, which can be more confusing than the words themselves. Most people come close enough to say the name correctly and be understood, even when the foreign words have sounds we don't have in English, like rolled *r*s or the *n* at the end of French words that is nasalized or swallowed. The *a* in Sylvaner, for example, is halfway between *van* and *von*, while the French and Germans accent the word differently. Who cares, anyway? Purists and pedants. Even clerks, natives, and scholars say names wrongly. The wine's the thing.

Only a few words give real trouble. Here's a list of twenty that are most often mispronounced. If you master all these, you will be considered a linguist—and they make a good quiz for any experts around. Getting ten right is excellent, with a 50-point bonus for saying *Montrachet* the way it should be said. The stresses fall on the capitalized letters in the phonetic spellings.

Aloxe-Corton	ah-lohss cor-tawn
Amontillado	ah-mon-tee-YAH-doe
Brouilly	brew-yee
Chablis	shab-lee
Chambertin	shahm-bare-tan
Chambolle-Musigny	shahm-bole mews-een-yee
Clos de Vougeot	clo-duh-voo-zho
Côtes de Nuits	coat-duh-nwee
Fixin	fee-san
Graves	grahv
Manzanilla	mahn-thah-NEEL-yah
Meursault	mere-so
Montrachet	mawn-rah-shay
Pouilly-Fuissé	poo-yee fwee-say
Savoie	sah-vwa
Soave	SWAH-vay
Spätlese	SHPATE-lay-zuh
Sauternes	so-tairn
Trockenbeerenauslese	trawk-ken BARE-en OUSE-lay-zuh
Vinho Verde	VEEN-yo vairdge

The wine word most often mispronounced may be Montrachet; the middle *t* is silent, as in *often*.

The French stress syllables very lightly, with some emphasis on the final syllable, like shab-LEE for Chablis, but to American ears the syllables have almost equal force.

The Spanish make *z* sound like *th*, the double *l* takes the *y* sound in *you*, and the *s* is often lisped. The Germans run words together so that they look harder than they are, and *s* often takes the sound of *sh* and sometimes *z*; *ei* sounds like *i* and *ie* sounds like *e*. The Italians sound everything, especially vowels, and so it goes.

The wine's the thing, no matter how we pronounce it, and perhaps the most useful list of words to learn are those of ten noble vines. They are pronounced pretty much the same wherever they are grown, and their names on a label are assurance of a good wine. Look at the list that follows:

Cabernet Sauvignon	cab-air-nay so-veen-yawn
Chenin Blanc	sheh-nan blawn
Merlot	mare-lo
Nebbiolo	neb-be-O-lo
Pinot Noir	pee-no nwahr
Riesling	REECE-ling
San Giovese	san-jo-VAY-see
Sémillon	say-me-yawn
Sylvaner	sil-VAN-er (seel-va-nair in French)
Trebbiano	treb-BYAH-no

A common word usually mispronounced is the French one for wine steward, *sommelier*, which is so-mel-yay. And the scientific word for noble rot, which is *Edelfäule* in German and *pourriture noble* in French (AID-el-FOY-luh and poo-ree-ture no-bl), is *Botrytis cinerea* or bo-TREET-iss sin-air-EH-ah. When in doubt, ask the *restaurateur* (res-tor-ah-turr).

75 Why are all kosher wines so sweet?

They're not. A kosher wine is one whose production is supervised by a rabbi, and many wines could be so approved. In this country, sweet and syrupy wines were those first made in compliance with dietary laws and came to be popular. Wines from the Israeli cooperatives are marketed in the United States under the Carmel label. Many of them are dry and made from such noble grapes as Cabernet Sauvignon and Chardonnay. A wide variety is generally available.

76 Does the shape of the bottle mean anything?

The great regions developed traditional bottle shapes: High-shouldered bottles are used for Bordeaux, bottles with sloping shoulders are used for Burgundy. Tall, slim bottles are used for Rhine wines.

Lesser regions adopted the same shapes to take advantage of the familiarity.

Dark glass is used to keep damaging light away from the wine, the best color being a greenish brown that is unattractive but practical. Clear glass is used for wines meant to be drunk promptly. Indented bases are used to make space for any sediment to settle, so that it will not flow into the wine when the bottle is poured. The hole is called the *punt* and it is considered stylish to hold the bottle with the thumb in the punt and the fingers spread on the bottle, when pouring. This is easy to do, but unnecessary.

77 Is it true that many good wines simply won't travel?

Some wines taste best straight from the cask, like the lightest Beaujolais, which loses freshness when it is put in bottle. Many light wines can be shipped today, because of better winemaking techniques.

A generation ago, only sturdy wines protected by fairly high alcohol—at least 12 percent—could withstand the jiggling and the temperature changes of shipping to market. These were usually the best wines of a region, those that improved with time in bottle. Americans got used to these big, robust wines that could spend perhaps a year on store shelves. When insulated containers came to be used for shipping, and as wines moved quickly through trade channels—sometimes a matter of weeks from cellar to table—it became possible to ship more fragile wines. Some of them are scarcely 11 percent alcohol, and yet they can travel safely. A large group of them are now available, light European whites and fruity reds that are quickly fermented. They have become quickly popular, and American vintners have begun producing similar wines. The alcoholic content is printed on the label; look for those that are 11 percent.

78 *Could you sum up for me some of the information you have told me to look for on a wine label?*

The best wines are vineyard wines—those that go to market bearing vineyard names—but there are too many to remember.

It's all very well to say the more specific the label the better the wine is apt to be. Innocent consumers need help.

The better European wines come under control laws and this is indicated on the bottle: *Appellation Contrôlée* identifies the top 20 percent of French wines; a stamp with VDQS appears on labels of another 10 percent. (The phrase means *Vins Delimités de Qualité Supérieure.*)

DOC identifies the best Italian wines. (*Denominazione di Origine Controllata.*)

These phrases appear on labels and guarantee authenticity. Other countries have similar laws, but identifying marks may not appear on labels.

The best wines are easy to buy. Burgundies will bear the phrase *Grand Cru* or *Premier Cru;* Bordeaux will bear the phrase *Cru Classé;* German wines will bear the phrase *Kabinett.* (Sweet German wines will bear one of the following words, which identify progressively sweeter wines: *Spätlese, Auslese, Beerenauslese, Trockenbeerenauslese.*)

The glorious abundance of names means that a few of them must be memorized to be sure of getting good wines. Because California wines are known by grape names—Zinfandel and Petite Sirah, Cabernet Sauvignon and Pinot Noir, Chardonnay and White Riesling—these should become familiar. A dozen other grape names might as well be committed to memory. They can be looked for on labels.

There is much useful information on the strip label, and the names of shipper and importer will become familiar as you find one or another whose wines please you. The back label, too, may give you much information about a wine.

The most useful thing to note about a label, though, comes after you have drunk the wine. If the wine was good, save the label, so you can buy another bottle without memorizing anything.

79 *People returning from Europe fondly remember marvelously pleasant wines served in carafes in little restaurants or bought from the barrel in country stores. Why can't we get wines like that?*

You're talking about wines drunk in the countryside where the grapes are grown—*vin de pays*—open wine, gone before the next vintage. If bottled at all, it is only long enough to get them to market, where they are drunk within days before they develop what is called bottle staleness.

Wines that can withstand a few weeks in bottle can be marketed, but rarely are, because today's customers demand wines that are crystal clear and free of floating particles. Such wines require filtering, which takes away some of their freshness and guts. "When people no longer demand wines that are completely clear we can make them," declares Myron Nightingale, veteran California winemaker. Motes in suspension in the wine, crystals of tartrates in the bottom of the bottle or on the cork, do not harm a wine at all; getting such things out of a wine does. Be on the look-out for such wines. Avoid, however, wines that are cloudy—a sign that there is something wrong with the wine.

80 *Can red wines be served chilled?*

Many are better when cool to the mouth, particularly young wines, and all inexpensive wines, like jug wines and blends with regional names. Cool is considered to be cellar temperature, which is somewhere between 50°F. and 55°F. (or 10°–12°C.). Cooling can blunt the taste of wines, which can be a good thing for cheap wines, serving to hide defects; but chilling can completely numb the taste of a wine. When a wine seems too cold, it can be allowed to warm up in the glass, usually a matter of a couple of minutes. Light reds like Beaujolais or Valpolicella may taste better after being left for an hour on the lowest shelf of the refrigerator.

81 *Just what is room temperature, anyway?*

Somewhere in the mid-sixties. Before central heating, European rooms were much cooler than they are today, and wines were brought from cold cellars to lose their chill. A wine at room temperature will taste cool in the mouth. There's no need to fuss with thermometers; a short time in a cool place or on a windowsill will bring a wine to a pleasing coolness.

Questions I Have Been Ashamed to Ask

82 *Sometimes I feel my questions are dumb—or too basic—to ask a wine expert. But I want the answers, anyway. For instance, just what is a regional wine?*

Questions are never dumb, although answers can be. Questions are usually about the problem of getting good wines on the table, how to buy them and serve them. The answers usually suggest several wines from different places, to give you a choice because every wine isn't in every market; therefore, answers may seem too detailed.

Wines came to be known by the places from which they came, because geography made the differences.

Regional wines are blends that are produced and distributed in quantity. The word is loosely used to identify all wines that are not from individual vineyards.

REGION	DISTRICT	TOWNSHIP OR COMMUNE
Burgundy	Côte de Beaune	Beaune, Volnay, Meursault, etc.
Bordeaux	Médoc	Margaux, Saint Julien, Pauillac, etc.
Rhineland	Moselle	Bernkastel, Piesport, Wehlen, etc.
California	Sonoma	Alexander Valley, Dry Creek, etc.
Italy	Piedmont	Barolo, Gattinara, Barbaresco, etc.

Wines labeled with district or township names like those above are casually termed *regional wines* by the trade.

83 *What does the word* vintage *really mean? Sometimes it seems to mean the year the wine was made, and sometimes, as with Port and Champagne, it seems to imply high quality.*

Vintage is the grape harvest and the wines made from it. Many wines carry the vintage year on the label to indicate how old the wine is. In the great regions, a vintage date on the label means that all the wine is from that particular harvest, an important consideration because the great Burgundies and Bordeaux and Rhines vary from year to year and take time to develop. You need to know the date so that you will not drink the wine before it is ready. For other wines, the date is important mostly to insure not drinking the wine too late, after it has faded.

Most wine districts permit the wines of a particular vintage to be "rationalized"—a euphemism for blending in wines of another year—to build up a thin wine with a coarse one, or whatever. Usually, not more than 25 percent of wine from another vintage can be added—if the vintage date is going to be used to market the wine. This blending is a desirable practice. Too many wines are sold as vintage wine because people think such wines are better than nonvintage wines. The reverse is almost always true. It is only when wines of a good vintage are stretched with lesser wines, resulting in a mediocre blend, that such mixing is to be deplored. Blending is a way to balance wines that may be undrinkable.

In many cases, the vintage date on a bottle has little or no significance. In the Rioja, for instance, it is common practice to refresh old wines with young, to round out young wines with old. The vintage on the label, the *cosecha*, may simply indicate the wine that was started with to make the blend.

This "refreshing" is common practice wherever wines are kept long in wood. In northern Italy, wines sometimes remain five years in wood, too long for modern tastes, even when small additions of young wine are made. Vintage dates on Piedmont and Valtellina wines can direct you to wines bottled three years or so after the vintage, made by modern methods. An older date would guide you to a woody wine in the classic tradition.

Vintage Ports are wines of exceptional years. The shipping firms declare a vintage, reserving a portion of the year's wine for bottling after two years in cask; these wines take fifteen years to round out, sometimes twice as long, many not being drunk until they are half a century old or older.

There is also a type called Late-Bottled Vintage Port, kept four years in cask, made generally from a vintage that will mature more rapidly than Vintage Port; late-bottlings are often drinkable within a decade of the vintage date. Tawny Ports sometimes carry a vintage date, quite meaningless, because the wines are regularly refreshed with younger wines as long as they are in cask.

This blending is essential for wines of the south, which vary greatly during their life in cask. (Brandy is often added to hold the wines to a desired taste.) Newly fermented wines for Spanish Sherry, for instance, are graded into types, then introduced into butts of older wines so that the young wines take on the character of the older. (See solera system, page 143.) For this reason Sherries can have no vintage, any date on the bottle being that of the setting up the tiers of butts used in the solera aging system.

Vintage Champagne has a somewhat special meaning, indicating that the wine is made from a particularly good harvest. A vintage Champagne is always much more expensive than the normal *cuvée* (the word means "vat" and is used to identify a particular blend), which is usually made up of several vintages. Most experts agree that few vintage Champagnes are worth the premium they command.

The wise wine buyer concentrates attention on vintages that produce large quantities of wine, so that a wide selection at competitive prices is available.

84 *What exactly does* premium wine *mean?*

Not very much. In the sixties, much wine from California was bulk wine or standard wine—large blends sold cheaply with European names. These California "Burgundies," "Chiantis," and "Rhines" came to be called generic wines, or types that were supposed to be like the European originals. They usually were not like them at all.

The growers of vineyards in the valleys of the coastal ranges wanted to set their wines apart from the generics. Their labels bore the names of the grapes, district names, even vintages—and they cost more and were better than the big blends. It was decided to call them premium wines. Premium is no longer much of an identifier of better wines; district and grape names on the label are your best leads to good wines.

85 *What does* generic *mean?*

A wine type. The term is used loosely to identify American wines with names borrowed from European regions, rather than brand names. (See above.)

86 *What does* vinifera *mean?*

Vinifera is the name that identifies wine grapes of Europe, as differentiated from native grapes. Crosses of the two varieties are called hybrids, and these are planted mostly in the East and Midwest, where they have begun producing good wines. They are called French-American hybrids, when the dominant grape is *vinifera.* Various *vinifera* grapes have been crossed with other *vinifera*—the Maréchal Foch is a cross of Pinot Noir and Gamay—and many of these show promise.

87 *Does a wine have to be old to be great?*

It has to be able to develop in the bottle. Wines that take ten years to develop taste bitter with tannin if tasted when they are only five years old, and they may have vegetable stenches or no smell at all, except a heavy alcoholic quality. These greatest of wines cost ten dollars a bottle when they first come on the market, three years after the vintage; then you have to wait. The temptation is strong to try a bottle after eight years. Finding it still bitter, you might try one the next year, and the next, and the wine may not taste just right until it is twenty years old—by that time, the case you bought is all gone. What's worse, if you buy such a great wine—it is called a *Grand Cru* in Burgundy, where a score of vineyards are entitled to be called a Great Growth—when it is ready to drink, it can cost twenty dollars and up and still not taste right because you don't know where it's been. Maybe it was stored in a warm cellar; maybe the cork leaked, or the bottle was shaken up.

Simple Questions That Wine Experts Like

88 Just how do you taste wines?

Two at a time, preferably, so you can compare. Wines tasted in pairs reveal things about each other. A wine tasted by itself may taste good, but tasted with another you can better decide if it is full or light, developed or too young. Differences are revealed, and you discover what you like about both.

89 What do I have to do to get to enjoy wines?

Simply taste them, regularly and casually. Familiarity breeds enjoyment. Wines vary so much from place to place that a description pinpoints its geography, not necessarily its place in the scheme of things. Wine talk, too, is confusing. Simply tasting—with foods you like—bypasses all the descriptions. Wines are good, familiar creatures, as St. Paul said. Wines are not to be taken too seriously, not even seriously at all, no more so than good cheese or good bread.

90 How do you recognize a good wine store?

There is one absolute and infallible rule for recognizing a good wine store, plain or fancy, large or small. There will be many bottles in the $4 to $5 price range prominently displayed, as if the owner were pointing these out to you as his discoveries.

Any store can stock a few bottles of expensive wines and many of those that are well advertised and/or cheap and popular. Good wines under $50 for a case of 12 are hard to find. Their presence on the shelf indicates that the staff has sought out the wines, tasted them, and is eager for you to try them.

A sad fact of life is that big stores with large volume can buy in large lots at better prices than neighborhood shops, however dedicated the owners might be. Shop your neighborhood store for special finds, but shop the big stores, too, for bargains. Enthusiastic wine drinkers spread their attention among three or four stores, also checking ads and new stores that may have something unusual.

A sure sign of a good store is that bottles are easy to find, carefully arranged by country and region. The most expensive wines—and the cheapest—should not be the ones most prominently displayed. As part of this matter of price, the best stores make comparisons easy by legible markings. (A dubious practice in second-rate stores is to jumble wines together, putting high-priced wines in prominent places, so that comparison is hard: in their ads, for instance, they will run good vintages with poor and mix up prices to confuse.)

Wines will be lying down, of course, so corks will stay wet, only the odd display bottle standing up on shelves or counters.

A sure way to check out a store is to ask for suggestions of wines from a particular region. If the wine offered is high in price compared to others from the same region, the store should be avoided.

Buy wines at off times during the day, so that the staff will have time to talk and explain their wines. If the staff is evasive, pompous, abrupt, or unknowing, find another store.

Tell Me More About Wine

Exceptional Champagnes

Burgundy Vineyards

Bordeaux Vineyards

German Regionals

California Regions

Wineries of New York and Elsewhere

Fortified Wines:
Sherry and Port (Porto)

Classic Wine-Food Affinities

Exceptional Champagnes

All the major Champagne houses produce special *cuvées,* blends of wines they consider particularly good, that are particularly distinguished by being high in price. Undoubtedly these wines are exceptional, but there are those that would prefer two bottles of nonvintage *Brut* or *Extra Sec* for the same price. For the extravagant, here is a list of these special Champagnes.

HOUSE	BRAND
Bollinger	RD
Canard Duchêne	Charles VII
Charles Heidsieck	Royal
Deutz & Gelderman	William Deutz
Heidsieck Monopole	Diamant Bleu
Krug	Blanc de Blancs
Lanson	Red Label
Laurent Perrier	Grand Siècle
Louis Roederer	Cristal
Moët et Chandon	Dom Pérignon
Mumm	René Lalou
Perrier-Jouët	Fleur de France
Piper-Heidsieck	Florens Louis
Pol Roger	Blanc de Chardonnay
Ruinart	Dom Ruinart
Taittinger	Comtes de Champagne
Veuve Clicquot-Ponsardin	La Grande Dame

To buy Burgundy's greatest wines, you need to know something of the geography in order to choose wines from specific vineyards, in preference to lesser blends marketed under township names.

Nobody knows why one strip of vineyard will produce wines better than the plot adjoining, but it is the basic fact of wine, nowhere more so than in Burgundy. That's why vineyard names are important and why there are so many of them. They are called *climats,* the climates changing with slight variations of soil, the way the sun hits, the way the land drains, and how air flows over the vines.

The best vineyards are in the curve of land where the plain meets the rise of the Golden Slope, the Cote d'Or—a thirty-mile stretch of vineyard that is the heart of Burgundy. Scarcely two dozen vineyards are legally called *Grand Cru,* "Great Growth," and perhaps there should be two score or more, but the laws are slow to change.

Ranked below them—often as good but not as long lasting (perhaps only ten years instead of twenty)—are the First Growths, perhaps two hundred vineyards entitled to be called *Premier Cru.* They are names to look for—and to check against official lists because shippers have been known to make up names that sound like vineyard names. (Wines from ordinary vineyards out in the plain usually go to market under the name of the township, which frequently takes the name of its greatest vineyard to its own to confuse you. The town of Gevrey is officially Gevrey-Chambertin, the second name being that of its greatest vineyard.)

Burgundy vineyards are divided among several owners, and the wines can vary so much that it is even hard to generalize them. The largest is Clos de Vougeot, a *Grand Cru* of 125 acres and some 60 owners, each of whom makes wine in his own way. A grower may own parts of several vineyards—a few vines in several First Growths in a township, for instance—and he may blend these to market a single wine that is called *Premier Cru,* without a vineyard name. It can often be a splendid wine.

The most distinctive wines are those bottled by the owner. The system is called estate-bottling, patterned after the custom in Bordeaux and along the Rhine, and is a guarantee of authenticity—and usually of quality. Shippers buy as much of the great wines as they can and are constantly accused of stretching the wines, which happens.

All this seems like more than you need to know. It is not. First Growths can cost more than $15 a bottle; Great Growths twice as much. And at those prices you don't want disappointing fakes—or even the overpriced wines with township names that compare not at all with genuine estate-bottled wines and those from distinguished shippers.

Burgundy is rare. Nearly half of it all is sold as Beaujolais, nearly a third more is sold as Mâcon, Bourgogne, Bourgogne Aligoté, Pinot Noir or Chardonnay, or a mélange called *passe-tout-grains.* Less than 20 percent of Burgundy's 25 million cases or so (less than 2 percent of French production in a good year) goes to market with the names that make Burgundy famous.

Ratings Wines are frequently rated on a scale of 20; 14 being good; 15–17 being very good to great; 18–20 being very great to outstanding. Here, 18/20, the 18 refers to the few best of the lesser wines, the 20 to the best of the First Growths and Great Growths; anyway, the numbers indicate a range of excellence.

Vintages:

1979. Spotty. Generally small production of some good wines. 14/16

1978 and 1977. Some good wines. 14/16

1976 and 1970. Large production of many great wines. 18/20

1975. Small production of many good, light wines from the best vineyards. 15/17

1974 and 1973. Large production of good, light wines from the best vineyards. 15/17

1972 and 1971. Small production of many great wines. 18/20

First Growths may be ready to drink four years after the vintage and stay at their primes for twice that time. Great Growths may take eight years to develop and last for twice as long.

The First Growths and the Great Growths in the lists that follow are a select sampling of vineyard names considered to be the best.

CÔTE DE NUITS

All but one of the red *Grands Crus* come from the Côte de Nuits, the northern half of the Golden Slope. Vineyards extend for a dozen miles—producing all red wines, among the world's greatest. (A few cases of white wine are made, scarcely in commercial quantities—Musigny Blanc, Clos Blanc de Vougeot—rarely to be found.)

The Great Growths are limited and rare and always expensive—and usually drunk before they have matured by people who insist on the best but can't wait. The wines can cost $30 and more when ready to drink, often ten years after the vintage.

The First Growths, usually ready to drink five years after the vintage, often cost $20.

The third group are wines marketed with the name of the township (Gevrey-Chambertin, for example) and can cost as much as vineyard wines, and may or may not be worth it, depending on the shipper. The best of them are usually Vosne-Romanée and Nuits-Saint-Georges.

A regional blend is marketed as *Vins Fins de la Côte de Nuits,* often a good buy at less than $10.

FIXIN

The wines of Fixin (pronounced "fee-san"), like their famous neighbors, the Chambertins, are full and only slightly less glorious—and usually much cheaper because they are not as well known as other Burgundies.

Clos de la Perrière	Les Hervelets
Clos du Chapitre	Clos du Napoléon
Les Arvelets	

Note: Only five vineyards are rated *Premier Cru,* the rest going to market as a regional blend, *Vins Fins de la Côte de Nuits,* also often a good buy.

GEVREY-CHAMBERTIN

Chambertins are noted for depth of flavor, color so dark it is called the robe, bouquet so intense it warrants the taster's term of nose. They are truly noble wines.

Monks established Clos de Bèze in the seventh century. A peasant named Bertin planted a field outside the walls, and both vineyards made the fame of Gevrey. Seven vineyards around the two are allowed to add Chambertin to their names. All are rated *Grand Cru.* A score are more or less officially rated *Premier Cru,* among them Clos Saint Jacques and Les Varoilles, underrated and therefore often exceptional buys.

Here are the *Grand Crus* and *Premiers Crus,* generally considered best.

CHAMBERTIN-CLOS DE BÈZE*	Clos Saint Jacques
CHAMBERTIN	Les Varoilles
LATRICIÈRES-CHAMBERTIN	Cazetiers
MAZIS-CHAMBERTIN	Aux Combottes
CHARMES- (OR MAZOYÈRES-) CHAMBERTIN	Combe aux Moines
CHAPELLE-CHAMBERTIN	
RUCHOTTES-CHAMBERTIN	
GRIOTTE-CHAMBERTIN	

*Great Growths are listed in capitals.

Note: Wines from minor vineyards, sold as Gevrey-Chambertin, are rarely equals of the better vineyard wines—but often cost as much, banking on the name instead of quality.

MOREY-SAINT-DENIS

With lordly Chambertins to the north and queenly Musignys to the south, the princely wines of Morey take after both. They were once marketed as wines of the neighboring townships, and so are less known and often less costly. The commune has some two dozen First Growths. Those listed are considered best.

CLOS DE TART*	Les Ruchots
CLOS DE LA ROCHE	Sorbet or Clos Sorbet
CLOS SAINT-DENIS	Les Millandes
BONNES MARES	Clos des Ormes
Clos des Lambrays	Monts-Luisants

Note: Clos des Lambrays is ranked with the *Grand Crus* of the town, and is the best of two dozen First Growths, but official rating has not yet been granted. (Part of Bonnes Mares is in the town, and it has the light elegance of the Musignys, as does Clos Saint-Denis.)

CHAMBOLLE-MUSIGNY

Musigny and its neighbors are light and elegant wines of great charm.

BONNES MARES*	Les Baudes
MUSIGNY	Combe d'Orveau
Les Amoureuses	Les Cras
Les Charmes	Les Sentiers

*Great Growths are listed in capitals.

Note: Les Amoureuses and Les Charmes are considered the best of a score of First Growths.

VOUGEOT

With some sixty owners of the 125 acres of Clos de Vougeot, all making wines in their own ways, the best summary is to say that these full wines of the walled vineyard—the *clos*—have big bouquets, but quality varies.

Note: Sections behind the great building are reputed best and have names like Grand or Petit Maupertuis, Montiottes Hautes, and Musigny de Clos Vougeot, occasionally found and always identified on back labels. There is some fine white wine outside the walls that surround the vineyards; other vineyards entitled to the name Vougeot, however, are not as good.

FLAGEY-ECHÉZEAUX

These have great finesse and elegance, like the neighboring Romanées.

GRANDS ECHÉZEAUX*   ECHÉZEAUX

Note: The First Growths of Flagey are marketed as Vosne-Romanées.

VOSNE-ROMANÉE

The Romanées are the most famous of Burgundies and the most expensive; velvety, with great finesse and unmatched balance. The

*Great Growths are listed in capitals.

Premiers Crus in the list that follows will have on the label the words Vosne-Romanée before the vineyard name.

ROMANÉE-CONTI*   Les Malconsorts
LA TÂCHE   Les Suchots
ROMANÉE SAINT-VIVANT   Les Beaux-Monts
RICHEBOURG   Les Petits-Monts
LA ROMANÉE   Aux Brulées
La Grande Rue

Note: Even wines labeled simply Vosne-Romanée are of superior quality, easily the best town wines of Burgundy.

NUITS-SAINT-GEORGES

The wines are robust and fill the mouth, being especially easy to drink and straightforward in taste. The following are the highly rated *Premiers Crus:*

Les Saint-Georges   Clos de la Maréchale**
Les Cailles   Clos Arlots
Les Vaucrains   Clos des Argillières
Les Pruliers   Clos des Grand Vignes
Les Porrets   Les Perdrix
Les Boudots   Clos des Forêts
Aux Murgers   Les Didiers
Clos de Thorey   Clos des Corvées

Note: The neighboring town of Prémeaux is allowed to sell its wines as Nuits-Saint-Georges. There are no Great Growths, but two score First Growths, and they often take six years or so to develop.

*Great Growths are listed in capitals.

**Clos de la Maréchale and vineyards following are in the township of Prémeaux.

The town wines often have a *goût de terroir,* an earth taste, not unpleasant.

CÔTE DE BEAUNE

Beaune is the capitol of the district it names—the southern half of the Golden Slope—a dozen miles of vineyard that produce excellent light reds and the greatest dry whites in the world. The only red ranked as a Greath Growth is Corton, (its white wine is ranked equally high) but many reds deserve higher ranking, particularly those of Volnay and Beaune itself. The whites ranked as Great Growths are the Montrachets, as well as Corton and Corton-Charlemagne; some of the white Meursault deserve higher ranking. They can cost $25.

The *Premiers Crus* have not all been ranked officially. The task is difficult because townships like Volnay produce wines far superior to those of Monthélie or Santenay, for instance. Burgundians dub the best vineyard of a commune as chief vats, or *Têtes de Cuvées.* (The phrase sometimes appears on a label and may indicate a superior wine.) Both reds and whites are often ready to drink when four years old and can cost $15 a bottle.

Wines marketed with only the town name can cost as much and are rarely worth it, perhaps with the exception of Volnay.

Blends of wines from minor towns are marketed as Côte de Beaune-Villages. Much of the wine from the following towns are so sold, and when half the price of wines with vineyard names, they're often good buys. Wines with only the township names can also be good buys when priced the same, around $10. Wines from these towns are worth looking for.

Auxey-Duresses	Monthélie
Pernand-Vergelesses	Santenay
Savigny-les-Beaune	Saint-Aubin

Various exceptional vineyards have been donated over the years to the charity hospital in Beaune—the Hospices de Beaune—and their wines are sold at their famous auction each year on the third Sunday of November. Buyers come from all over the world to buy the wines of the Hospices de Beaune, which are marketed under the name of the donor, as *Cuvée* so and so. Lots from each vineyard are sold by the *pièce*, equal to a barrel of 228 liters, 24 cases of 12 bottles each.

The wines set the prices for the current vintage and are usually high. The barrels are carted away for ageing and bottling, which is usually done satisfactorily. There are some thirty *cuvées* to choose from, the labels indicating the town or vineyard from which the wines come. Some of the famous *cuvées* are:

Corton:	Charlotte Dumay	Pommard:	Dames de la Charité
	Docteur Peste		Billardet
Beaune:	Nicolas Rolin	Volnay:	Blondeau
	Guigone de Salins		Général Muteau
Savigny:	Arthur Girard	Meursault:	Jehan Humblot
	Forquerand		

ALOXE-CORTON

Corton, a vineyard said to have been planted on orders from Charlemagne, is the only red wine in the Côte de Beaune of the two dozen Great Growths. (All the other *Grands Crus* of the Côte de Beaune are white.) The big wines are noted for outstanding balance and bouquet and are long lived, often taking a decade to develop and living twice as long. A third of the Corton vineyard produces a white wine that is a Great Growth, and is called Corton-Charlemagne.

CORTON	Corton-Perriers
Corton-Clos du Roi	Corton-Les Maréchaudes
Corton-Bressandes	Languettes
Corton-Renardes	Les Pougets

Note: The best vineyards have Corton preceding their names, over two dozen of which are being ranked as First Growths. The outstanding shipper, Louis Latour, blends his holdings in Corton to produce Corton Grancey, his brand name for a superior wine.

PERNAND-VERGELESSES

These are good Burgundies that are not too well known and can therefore be had at attractively low prices. The wines are light and fruity, but are usually passé after five years. Here are the *Premiers Crus*.

Ile des Vergelesses	Les Fichots
Les Basses Vergelesses	En Caradeux
Creux de la Net	

Note: Official listing of First Growths is slow. Much of the wine goes into good blends called Côte de Beaune-Villages.

BEAUNE

The soft, easy-to-drink wines of Burgundy's capitol and largest township are quenching and usually ready to drink four years after the vintage and stay at their primes for perhaps as long. Some three dozen vineyards are considered *Primiers Crus*. Look for these vineyard names in the list that follows:

Grèves	Clos du Roi
Fèves	Marconnets
	Les Avaux
Bressandes	Les Cras
Les Cent-Vignes	Aigrots
Champimonts	Clos de la Mousse
Clos des Mouches	Les Theurons

Note: Grèves and Fèves are *Premiers Crus* ranked above the others.

SAVIGNY-LES-BEAUNE

Light and elegant Savignys, quickly ready, can be drunk three years after the vintage and can be past their prime when only five years old.

Vergelesses	Jarrons
Marconnets	Dominode
Lavières	

Note: Vineyards listed are considered to produce the best wines.

POMMARD

The most famous wines of the Beaune Slope, these full and sturdy wines are priced well above their worth.

Rugiens, Bas or Hauts
Epenots or Petits Epenots

Pézerolles	Chanlins-Bas
Clos Blanc	Platière
Chanière	Arvelets
Charmot	Clos de la Commaraine

Note: Some two dozen vineyards are considered to be First Growths, and Rugiens and Epenots are ranked above the others.

VOLNAY

These are soft and fruity wines of great elegance, easy to drink. The best-known *Premiers Crus* are:

Caillerets	Chevret
Clos des Ducs	Clos des Chênes
Champans	Les Santenots
Fremiets	

Note: A dozen vineyards are considered First Growths. Red wines from neighboring Meursault are marketed as Volnay-Santenots.

MONTHÉLIE

Monthélie is Volnay's neighbor just up the hill. Its wines are like Volnay, but not as wonderful—and should cost a couple of dollars less a bottle. Look for these *Premiers Crus.*

Les Champs-Fulliot	Sur La Velle
La Taupine	Duresse

Note: Several other vineyards are considered First Growths. Most are marketed as Côte de Beaune-Villages.

AUXEY-DURESSES

The wines are like lesser Volnays, light and fragrant, good value when half the price of Volnay.

Les Duresses   Bas-des-Duresses

Note: Half a dozen vineyards are considered First Growths. Duresses is ranked best.

MEURSAULT

Meursault produces soft, dry white wines with a special fragrance that seems now and then nutty, with overtones of spring flowers. The wines have an open, ingratiating quality and are best when young, perhaps three or four years after the vintage. The wines age quickly, taking on the straw taste of maderization and a golden color—like the wines of Madeira. The best-known *Premiers Crus* are:

Perrières or Clos des Perrières   Charmes
Genevrières   Goutte d'Or

Note: Nearly a score of vineyards, including some from the neighboring hamlet of Blagny, are considered to be First Growths. The few reds are marketed as Volnay-Santenots.

PULIGNY-MONTRACHET (White Wines)

Puligny and the neighboring town of Chassagne enclose all five of the Great Growth vineyards entitled to the name of Montrachet. The Montrachets are almost universally considered to be the finest dry white wines in the world. Another claim to fame is that no name in wine is so often mispronounced, even in France. (The proper pronunciation is "mawn-rash-ay.")

Other vineyards in the township also produce superior white wines, the First Growths most often to be found being only slightly less glorious than the Montrachets.

LE MONTRACHET* (about half)
Chalumeaux
BÂTARD-MONTRACHET (about half)   Pucelles
CHEVALIER-MONTRACHET   Clavoillons
BIENVENUE-BÂTARD-MONTRACHET   Caillerets
Les Combettes   Folatières
Blagny

CHASSAGNE-MONTRACHET (White and Red Wines)

The firm, rounded wines of Chassagne develop a certain finesse, but are often past their prime at five years.

LE MONTRACHET* (about half)   Ruchottes
BATARD-MONTRACHET (about   Caillerets
   half)
CRIOTS-BÂTARD-MONTRACHET   Morgeot (also red wines)

Note: A dozen vineyards are considered First Growths, but most of these are marketed as Morgeot, a name that has become familiar.

There are also good First Growths of red wines that come from such vineyards as Clos Saint Jean, Bourdriotte, and Maltroie.

*Great Growths are listed in capitals.

SANTENAY

Santenay produces light and fruity wines ready to drink a few months after bottling—a wine to drink by quantity when the price is low.

LES GRAVIÈRES

Note: Like other minor Burgundy communes, most of the wines are sold in blends marketed as Côte de Beaune-Villages. Les Gravières is considered the best vineyard.

CHABLIS

The district just above the Golden Slope produces light and dry white wines that are among the most imitated. The imitations are never more than ordinary. There are seven Great Growths and a score of First Growths, wines vastly superior to those called simply Chablis. Wine marketed as Petit Chablis comes from a large area and is traditionally drunk in carafe.

VAUDÉSIR*	Mont de Milieu
GRENOUILLES	Montée de Tonnerre
LES CLOS	Fourchaume
VALMUR	Vaucoupin
LES PREUSES	Vaillons
BLANCHOTS	Montmain
BOURGROS	Côte de Lechet
	Beauroy
	Vosgros
	Melinots
	Les Fourneaux

*Great Growths are listed in capitals.

Note: Chablis is the traditional wine to serve with oysters, but it is good with fish and seafood simply prepared and is a superb wine to drink by itself, before a meal.

SOUTHERN BURGUNDY

Southern Burgundy encompasses three districts—Beaujolais, Mâconnais, and Chalonnais—producing wines that are not ranked as highly as those from the Golden Slope and Chablis. They are good buys when priced under $6.

CÔTE CHALONNAISE

The district just below the Golden Slope produces mostly fresh and light white wines from the communes of Montagny and Rully, light and fruity reds mostly from Mercurey and Givry. They are practically ready to drink when bottled, certainly within three years of the vintage. The wines are as delicious as their names, good buys when one-fourth less than Côte de Beaunes.

CÔTE MÂCONNAISE

This large district of southern Burgundy is noted for ten white wines that are fresh, light, and quenching, the best and best-known being Pouilly-Fuissé, which is greatly overpriced. Almost as good are its neighbors—Pouilly-Vinzelles and Pouilly-Loché, particularly when priced around $8. Still lower in price should be Saint Veran and the underrated wines of Viré, Lugny, and Clessé. Still lower in price are often-good whites sold as Pinot-Chardonnay-Mâcon and Mâcon Blanc. All of these are made from the Chardonnay grape, sometimes with a portion of Aligoté in the blends of the lesser wines, a grape whose name occasionally appears on labels. A coarse, often-pleasing red is Mâcon Rouge, which should be inexpensive. For quick reference, the following wines are listed in descending order of excellence.

WHITES	REDS
Pouilly-Fuissé	Mâcon Rouge
Pouilly-Vinzelles	
Pouilly-Loché	
Saint Véran	
Viré	
Lugny	
Clessé	
Pinot-Chardonnay-Mâcon	
Mâcon Blanc	
Aligoté	

Note: Pouilly-Fuissé and the other whites warrant that fond old wine cliché, "good but not great." These are wines for everyday drinking when priced around $6. Aligoté is the traditional wine for Kyr; a dollop of the currant liqueur, Cassis, is poured in a glass, then filled with the wine; pretentious restaurants use Champagne instead of Aligoté.

BEAUJOLAIS

Beaujolais is the pet young wine of French restaurants, fruity and fresh and not so authoritative as to detract from the food. Wines simply called *Beaujolais* are rarely more than ordinary; *Beaujolais Supérieur* is not much better. *Beaujolais-Villages*, a blend from the various *communes*, is generally good.

A fast vinification of lesser wines is rushed to Paris on November 15 to herald the new vintage and this *Beaujolais Nouveau* is often lacking the characteristic fruitiness, having to be well filtered to be drinkable. Wine bottled promptly after fermentation reaches Paris with the new year; it is called *Beaujolais Primeur* and can be good when not manhandled. The most delightful Beaujolais is meant to be drunk up before the next vintage, preferably straight from the barrel, and this is called *Beaujolais de l'Année*.

Some Beaujolais taste best the second year after the vintage, notably those from the communes of Morgon, Moulin-à-Vent, Chénas, and Juliénas. The rest should be drunk as soon as possible, preferably from the cask. Chiroubles is often ready by Valentine's Day, followed quickly by the others. There are nine recognized Beaujolais growths, but many are now high in price, often $8. Beaujolais is a victim of inflation.

Look for wines from these particular Beaujolais areas.

Chiroubles	Julienas
Fleurie	Chenas
Saint-Amour	Moulin-à-Vent
Brouilly	Morgon
Côte de Brouilly	

Note: Chiroubles is rarely exported; Fleurie is so delightful most of it is drunk in France. The rest come here and are usually delicious.

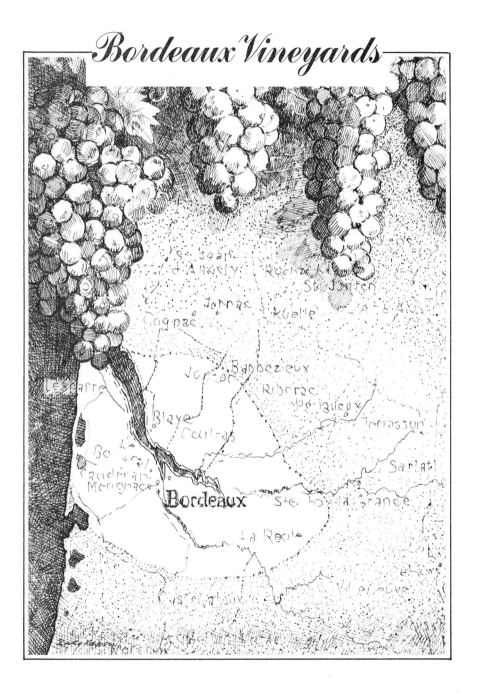

Bordeaux Vineyards

In the lists given here, the Classed Growths are the vineyards considered to be the best in the commune.

OUTSTANDING GROWTHS
(*CRUS HORS CLASSÉS*)

The eight Bordeaux vineyards listed below are rated so far above the other classifications that they cost twice as much as those from neighboring vineyards that are only slightly less good. Prices start around $12 a bottle, even in an ordinary year. In a good year, prices may be half as much again—for wines that will not become drinkable until ten years after the vintage; then they may cost $30 a bottle or more. Most of these great wines are drunk long before they are ready; the 1975 vintage, for instance, will just begin coming into its prime in the 1990s in time to welcome the new century. Vintages of '70 and '71 are in the same class—but many of the wines have already been drunk.

The Great Growths are:

CHÂTEAU MARGAUX CHÂTEAU HAUT-BRION
CHÂTEAU LAFITE   CHÂTEAU AUSONE
CHÂTEAU MOUTON CHÂTEAU CHEVAL BLANC
CHÂTEAU LATOUR   CHÂTEAU PÉTRUS

MARGAUX

The wines of Margaux are generally considered to be the lightest and most elegant of all those of Bordeaux, with fine bouquets. The township is large, made larger by the fact that neighboring *communes*—Cantenac, Soussans, Labarde, and Arsac—can be marketed as Margaux. Some of the best Bordeaux buys come from the little-known nearby towns of Moulis, Listrac, and others, whose vine-yards are rated as *Crus Exceptionnels* or *Crus Bourgeois;* these wines should cost less than $6, but like those from Margaux, may take a decade to mature in a year rated as good.

The outstanding vineyard of Margaux, officially rated as *Premier Grand Cru,* is Château Margaux. It can take twice as long to develop. Classed Growths of Margaux may cost $8 in a good year, right after the vintage, when they are offered for future delivery. When first shipped, usually three years after the vintage, they may cost twice that, even though the buyer may have to wait another decade before the wines are at their best. Ten years after the vintage, when the wine may be scarcely ready to drink, bottles can cost $20 and up.

CHÂTEAU MARGAUX*	
Château Rausan-Ségla	Light, elegant
Château Rauzan-Gassies	Lighter, delicate
Château Lascombes	Fine bouquet
Château Brane-Cantenac	Big, well-balanced
Château Cantenac-Brown	Big, with breed
Château Boyd-Cantenac	Light, elegant
Château d'Issan	Breed and finesse
Château Palmer	Balanced, elegant
Château Malescot-Saint-Exupéry	Elegant, fine
Château Marquis-d'Alesme-Becker	A lesser wine
Château Kirwan	A lesser wine
Château Giscours	Delicate, soft
Château Marquis-de-Terme	Full and rich
Château Prieuré-Lichine	Fast-maturing
Château Pouget	Second wine of Boyd-Cantenac

*Great Growths are listed in capitals.

SAINT JULIEN

Saint Juliens are considered to be fuller than those of Margaux, and softer, making them the first of the Médocs to become ready to drink—eight or ten years instead of a dozen or a score. There is a lot of wine from lesser vineyards, blended into regionals marketed as Saint Julien, generally good values at about $6, worth tasting now and then when you want to see how a vintage is coming along. The following Classed Growths can cost $10 and even more:

Château Gruaud-Larose	Fruity, fast-maturing
Château Léoville-Poyferré	Fullest of the Léovilles, fine
Château Léoville-Las-Cases	Well-balanced, good
Château Léoville-Barton	Good, well-balanced
Château Langoa-Barton	Typical, good, light
Château Beychevelle	Rounded, elegant
Château Talbot	Sturdy, full, slow-maturing
Château Gloria	Full, rounded, one of the best
Château Ducru-Beaucaillou	Rich, slow-maturing
Château Brainaire-Ducru	Robust
Château Lagrange	Slow-maturing, coarse

PAUILLAC

Dominated by Lafite, Mouton, and Latour, the balanced, full and fruity wines from the other Classed Growths of the township are often considered to be secondary when they get to market. The vineyards of Pauillac produce the most consistent and subtly grand of all Bordeaux wines, needing well over ten years to develop in good years and continuing to be drinkable for a decade and even longer. Like Mouton, many of them seem uninteresting and dull while still developing, but no wines so richly reward the patient.

The Great and Classed Growths are:

CHÂTEAU LAFITE-ROTHSCHILD*
CHÂTEAU LATOUR
CHÂTEAU MOUTON-ROTHSCHILD

Château Pichon-Longueville-Baron	Full, balanced
Château Pichon-Longueville-Lalande	Fruity, lighter
Château Duhart-Milon	Part of Lafite domain, overpriced but decent
Château Clerc-Milon	Part of Mouton domain, full
Château Mouton-Baron-Philippe	Part of Mouton, rounded
Château Pontet-Canet	Largest Médoc château, near Mouton
Château Grand-Puy-Lacoste	Balanced, elegant
Château Grand-Puy Ducasse	Lighter, with finesse
Château Lynch-Moussas	Rich, quick-maturing
Château Lynch-Bages	Rich, intense
Château Haut-Bages-Liberal	Full, powerful
Château Croizet-Bages	Good, full
Château Batailley	Good, typical
Château Haut-Batailley	Typical, good
Château Pedesclaux	Little known, little honored

SAINT ESTEPHE

The full, big wines of Saint Estèphe are the easiest of the Médocs to drink, straightforward and generous. There are many good vineyards, besides those of the Classed Growths, and the regionals are good buys. The lesser wines sometimes have an earthy taste, not unplea-

*Great Growths are listed in capitals.

sant, and many prefer to drink the wines before they are too ancient and still have a certain sturdiness about them—when they are nearer ten years old than twenty.

Château Cos d'Estournel	Fine, sturdy, perhaps lightest
Château Montrose	Long-lived, full
Château Calon-Ségur	Robust, long-lived
Château de Pez	Opposite Calon-Segur, full
Château Lafon-Rochet	Sturdy, near Pauillac, complex
Château Cos-Labory	Big, long-lived
Château Phélan Segur	Long-lived, big
Château Meyney	Typical
Château Marbuzet	Typical

GRAVES

These are sturdy, forthright wines that have great subtlety in good years that have been well kept for a decade and more. Wines from lesser vineyards seem to become harsh and thin with age but are appealing when less than ten years old. Haut-Brion is good when young (even at four years) and also in off years, and its neighbors are similar. Château Couhins and Laville-Haut-Brion produce rated white wines.

CHÂTEAU HAUT-BRION*	
Château La Mission Haut-Brion	Velvety, generous
Château Pape-Clément	Fine, full
Château La Tour-Haut-Brion	Hard to find, good
Château La Tour-Martillac (red and white)	Sturdy, hard to find
Château Smith-Haut-Lafite	Firm
Château Bouscaut (red and white)	Good, typical

*Great Growths are listed in capitals.

Château Haut-Bailly	Long-lived, sturdy, balanced
Domaine de Chevalier	Full, long-lived
Château de Fieuzal	Superior, fine
Château Carbonnieux (red and white)	Elegant, dry
Château Malartic-Lagravière	Full, 75 percent Cabernet Sauvignon
Château Olivier (red and white)	Mostly white, typical Graves; pleasant red

SAINT-EMILION

Official ratings are not easy to set up because nobody wants to be less than best and people buy by lists. Sainte-Emilion growers finally accepted ratings in 1955 that listed a dozen vineyards as *Premier Grand Cru Classé*, dozens of others as *Grand Crus Classés*, with Château Ausone and Château Cheval Blanc leading all the rest. Some sixty more are ranked as *Grands Crus*. The ratings appear on the labels, but bear in mind that there are many other excellent wines, fighting for recognition and offering excellent values at $6 or even less. The wines are generally fruity, balanced—and varying.

CHÂTEAU CHEVAL BLANC*	
CHÂTEAU AUSONE	
Château Belair (or Bel-Air)	Owned by adjoining Ausone; similar
Château Magdelaine	Distinctive, full
Château Canon	Generous, full, with breed
Clos Fourtet	Full, typical *Premier Grand Cru*
Château Beauséjour-Becot	Near Canon & Fourtet, light, fine

*Great Growths are listed in capitals.

Château Beauséjour-Duffau	Light, rounded
Château La Gaffelière	Ranks with Cheval Blanc, balanced
Château Figeac	Sturdy, soft, typical
Château Croque-Michotte	Typical of *Grand Cru* vineyards
Château Pavie	Large vineyard, big bouquet, full
Château Ripeau	Full; near Cheval Blanc and like it
Château Trottevielle	Big body, deep color
Château l'Angelus	Balanced, soft, fast-maturing
Château Troplong-Mondot	Large vineyard, typical wine, balanced
Château La Tour-du-Pin-Figeac	Adjoins Figeac; similar
Château Corbin (Gonaud)	Large vineyard, now several; near Cheval Blanc and like it

POMEROL

A small district, but perhaps none offers so many good wines so consistently. The Merlot is the most popular grape, producing soft and rounded wines that can be ready to drink in five years, although an outstanding vineyard, and its neighbors, like Pétrus or l'Evangile, can be at their best when twenty years old. Even the lesser vineyards, however, may not reach their primes in ten years. The vineyards have never been classified officially, but all 1,500 acres produce distinguished wines, Château Pétrus is considered greatest of all.

CHÂTEAU PÉTRUS*

Château Vieux-Château-Certan	Velvety, sturdy, consistent
Château Certan	Typical, once part of Certan
Château La Conseillante	Full, near and like Cheval Blanc

*Great Growths are listed in capitals.

Château Beauregard	The only good one of this name
Château l'Evangile	Excellent, typical, full
Château La Fleur	Good, but hard to find
Château La Fleur-Pétrus	Typical, but hard to find
Château Gazin	Full, balanced
Château Latour-Pomerol	Part of Pétrus domain; full, good
Château Nénin	Fruity, soft; one of the largest
Château Petit-Village	Firm, long-lived, distinctive
Château La Pointe	Full, sturdy, generous
Clos René	Lighter, but good

PETITS CHÂTEAUX & MINOR DISTRICTS

Some 70,000 vineyards in Bordeaux meet the requirements of the control laws. Their red wines are called clarets by the English, to simplify matters; the vineyards are called châteaux by the French to add tone, and the trade has adopted both words to make the wines appealing in the marketplace. Neither word is an indication of quality.

Some 100 vineyards appear in all the lists above, rated the best and called *Crus Classés*. They command the highest prices. Another 100 or so are ranked just below them, as *Crus Bourgeois*. (Sometimes added to the phrase are *Grand* or *Exceptionnel*, to make further distinctions.) These, and many others that command much lower prices, are called *Petits Châteaux* by the trade. Many of them are good buys.

Many of the good Petits Châteaux are entitled only to the ranking of *Bordeaux Supérieur* under the laws of *Appellation Contrôlée*. Other good clarets are identified only by the name of the small districts from which they come. There is no need to search for château names on the official lists, but look for the names on labels of the small districts listed below, roughly in order of quality. The clarets should not cost more than $5 and are usually ready to drink four years after the vintage.

Lalande de Pomerol
Canon-Fronsac or Côtes-Canon-Fronsac
Montagne-Saint-Emilion or Puisseguin-Saint-Emilion
Côtes de Bourg or Bourgeais

SAUTERNES

Sauternes and the towns that make up the district, like Barsac, produce sweet and luscious wines. Even the lesser château-bottlings are excellent (see list on page 41), while the *Premiers Crus* are considered only slightly less fine than the *Premier Grand Cru* of Château d'Yquem.

CHÂTEAU D'YQUEM[*]   Château Coutet
Château La Tour Blanche   Château Climens
Château Lafaurie Peyraguey   Château Guiraud
Clos Haut-Peyraguey   Château Rieussec
Château de Rayne-Vigneau   Château Rabaud-Promis
Château Suduiraut   Château Rabaud-Sigalas

[*]Great Growths are listed in capitals.

German Regionals

Germans love lists even more than the French, and early in the seventies they decided to get rid of most of the 25,000 names in the eleven regions. It was decreed that vineyards must be at least a dozen acres from the same hill or slope or soil and be marketed with a common name, or *Grosslage*. This amounted to the Burgundy way of adding the most famous vineyard name in town to that of the town itself so that the lowliest wines could bear a grand name. The result was many more regional blends masquerading as vineyard wine.

The new decrees also designated a grade of regional wines that could be sugared to bring up their alcoholic content to 11 percent or so—sturdy enough for export. Ever optimistic, they were dubbed Quality Wines—*Qualitätswein*—to distinguish them from even lesser wines. They are equal to Côtes-du-Rhône or Beaujolais-Villages. Supposedly, the new regionals are better than the old ones. Here is a list of Grosslagen from the main districts.

MOSEL-SAAR-RUWER REGION

With its two tributaries, the Mosel has some 28,000 acres of vineyard, two-thirds of them Riesling. The best vineyards are in the Mittel-Mosel, those marked with three stars, providing more fine wines than those rated two stars. There are many others.

TOWNSHIPS	GROSSLAGEN
MOSEL	
***Piesporter	Michelsberg
** Brauneberger	Kurfürstlay
***Bernkasteler	Kurfürstlay or Badstube
***Graacher	Münzlay
***Wehlener	Münzlay
***Zeltinger	Münzlay

** Erdener	Schwarzlay
** Ürziger	Schwarzlay

SAAR
** Kanzemer	Scharzberg
***Wiltingener	Scharzberg
** Oberemmeler	Scharzberg
** Ockfener	Scharzberg

RUWER
** Maximin Grünhauser	Römerlay
** Eitelsbacher (or Trierer)	Römerlay

RHEINGAU REGIONALS *(GROSSLAGEN)*

There remain some vineyards so famous—Schloss Johannisberg, Schloss Vollrads, Steinberg—that they do not carry the town names, and there are others larger than a dozen acres that retain their names; they are called Einzellagen, "single vineyards," a word that will appear on the label. The Grosslagen, however, dominate the market and should be lower in price.

TOWNSHIPS	GROSSLAGEN
***Rudesheimer	Burgweg
**Geisenheimer	Erntebringer
***Johannisberger	Erntebringer
**Winkeler	Oberberg
**Hallgartener	Mehrhölzchen
***Hattenheimer	Deutelsberg
***Erbacher	Deutelsberg

**Kiedricher	Heiligenstock
***Rauenthaler	Steinmächer
***Eltviller	Eltviller
**Hochheimer	Daubhaus

RHEINHESSEN REGIONALS *(GROSSLAGEN)*

There are more than thirty thousand vineyard acres in Hessen, well over a third of them Müller-Thurgau, well over a quarter in Sylvaner and only about 5 percent in Riesling, which produces the best wines. Of the many towns, four deserve extra stars. Much wine at less than $5 a bottle is available, and worth trying in good years.

TOWNSHIPS	GROSSLAGEN
**Oppenheimer	Kröttenbrunnen or Güldenmorgen
***Niersteiner	Spiegelberg or Auflangen or Gutes Domtal
***Nackenheimer	Spiegelberg
**Bingener	Sankt Rochuskapelle

RHEINPFALZ REGIONALS *(GROSSLAGEN)*

With more than fifty thousand acres of vineyard, somewhat more than a quarter in Müller-Thurgau, somewhat less than a quarter in Sylvaner, the best wines come from the some ten square miles of Riesling. Of the many towns, four deserve noting, their regionals perhaps better than others and worth $4 or so in good years.

TOWNSHIPS	GROSSLAGEN
**Ruppertsberger	Hofstück
***Deidesheimer	Hofstück

***Forster   Mariengarten
**Wachenheimer   Schenkenböhl

NAHE REGIONALS *(GROSSLAGEN)*

Of the ten thousand acres, more than a third are in Müller-Thurgau, more than a quarter in Sylvaner, less than a quarter in Riesling, and many acres of experimental grapes, all worth trying. The wines are little known and should be cheaper than more famous ones, but their prices remain above \$4, rising much higher when vineyard wines are bought.

TOWNSHIPS	GROSSLAGEN
Schloss Böckelheimer	Rosengarten
Kreuznacher	Kronenberg

FRANKEN REGIONALS *(GROSSLAGEN)*

Steinwein from Franconia is one of Germany's best regionals, produced on some fifteen square miles of vineyard, of which nearly half is Müller-Thurgau and a third Sylvaner, with many experimental grapes to bring interest to the blends. Little of it comes here, perhaps because so much attention focusses on Liebfraumilch and companions. Würzburg, whose Stein vineyard gave its name to the regional wine, has no Grosslage, but those listed below are worth looking for.

TOWNSHIPS	GROSSLAGEN
Randersacker	Ewig Leben
Iphofener	Burgweg
Escherndorfer	Kirchberg
Rödelsee	Schlossberg

CALIFORNIA REGIONS
WINERIES AND SELECTIONS

California's best wines come from the slopes and the valleys of the coastal ranges around the San Francisco Bay area. The regions of the North Coast are Sonoma, Napa, and Mendocino, north of San Francisco, Santa Clara and Santa Cruz to the south, with San Benito forming what may best be called South Bay, with Livermore Valley to the east of the bay.

Still farther south are the counties that make up what is being called the Central Coast: San Benito and Monterey, San Luis Obispo, and Santa Barbara. The last two counties are sometimes defined as making up the Central Coast, the others tossed in with the North Coast. No matter. Listed below are premium producers that market more than ten thousand cases a year. Their wines are available in most major markets. Smaller wineries, many among the best producers, can be found in the largest markets, and a selective listing of these is included.

California has a Mediterranean climate in the coastal valleys where the weather is much milder than in the great wine regions like Bordeaux, Burgundy, and the Rhine, whose grapes grow in marginal conditions. Vines under stress seemed to produce grapes better for wine than when the same vines were grown farther south and received plenty of warmth, water, and nutrients. Californians questioned this idea, improving vineyard and winemaking techniques, many of which were quickly adopted around the world.

They also developed vines from the best grapes that were free of disease, stocks chosen to match the climate. Cabernet Sauvignon and Sauvignon Blanc from Bordeaux grew well, as did Chardonnay and other Burgundy grapes. The Riesling and Sylvaner of the Rhine thrived. So did two grapes that were *vinifera,* but not easy to trace to European sources: the Zinfandel (like a variety grown in southern Italy) and the Petite Sirah (like a minor grape of the Rhone, the

Duriff). Various crosses of noble varieties with standard producers were made. These were called mid-varietals, to distinguish them from the noble vines of the great districts.

For names of grapes to look for on labels, see the following list:

NAPA VALLEY

Grapes

WINERIES	REDS	WHITES
Beaulieu Vineyards (BV)	Cabernet Sauvignon	Johannisberg Riesling
Beringer Winery	Gamay Noir	Fumé Blanc
Burgess Cellars	Petite Sirah	Green Hungarian
Chappellet Vineyards	Cabernet Sauvignon	Chenin Blanc
Chateau Montelena	Cabernet Sauvignon	Chardonnay
Christian Brothers Winery	Red Pinot	Pinot Chardonnay
Clos du Val	Zinfandel, Cabernet Sauvignon	
Conn Creek Winery	Barbera	Sauvignon Vert
Cuvaison Cellars	Zinfandel	Chardonnay
Domaine Chandon		Pinot Noir Blanc
Franciscan Vineyards	Gamay	Chenin Blanc
Freemark Abbey Winery	Cabernet Sauvignon	Chardonnay
Heitz Wine Cellars	Cabernet Sauvignon	Chardonnay
Inglenook Vineyards	Zinfandel	Chenin Blanc
Hanns Kornell Cellars		Brut
Charles Krug Winery	Gamay Beaujolais	Chenin Blanc
Louis Martini Winery	Cabernet Sauvignon	Folle Blanche
Robert Mondavi Winery	Gamay	Fumé Blanc
Joseph Phelps Vineyards	Syrah	Johannisberg Riesling
Rutherford Hill	Pinot Noir	Chardonnay
Schramsberg Vineyards	Cuvée de Gamay	Blanc de Noir
Spring Mountain Vineyards	Cabernet Sauvignon	Sauvignon Blanc
Stag's Leap Wine Cellars	Cabernet Sauvignon	Chardonnay
Sterling Vineyards	Merlot	Chenin Blanc
Sutter Home Winery	Zinfandel	

SONOMA VALLEY

Grapes

WINERIES	REDS	WHITES
Buena Vista	Zinfandel	Green Hungarian
Chateau St. Jean	Cabernet Sauvignon	Pinot Blanc
Davis Bynum Winery	Merlot	French Colombard
Dry Creek Vineyard	Gamay Beaujolais	Fume Blanc
Geyser Peak Winery	Cabernet Rosé	Chardonnay
Grand Cru Vineyards	Zinfandel	Gewürztraminer
Italian Swiss Colony	Zinfandel	Green Hungarian
Kenwood Vineyards	Petite Sirah	Chenin Blanc
Korbel & Bros.	Cabernet Sauvignon	Sonoma Blanc
Pedroncelli Winery	Cabernet Sauvignon	Chardonnay
Sausal Winery	Gamay, Zinfandel	
Sebastiani Vineyards	Nouveau Gamay, Barbera	
Simi Winery	Gamay Beaujolais	Chardonnay
Sonoma Vineyards	Cabernet Sauvignon	Johannisberg Riesling
Souverain Cellars	Zinfandel	Chenin Blanc
Trentadue Winery	Zinfandel	Chenin Blanc

MENDOCINO

Grapes

WINERIES	REDS	WHITES
Cresta Blanca	Zinfandel	Chenin Blanc
Parducci	Petite Sirah	French Colombard
Fetzer Vineyards	Carmine Carignane	Blanc de Blancs
Weibel Wine Cellars	Gamay Beaujolais	Chardonnay Brut

LIVERMORE VALLEY

Grapes

WINERIES	REDS	WHITES
Concannon Vineyard	Petite Sirah	Sauvignon Blanc
Stony Ridge Winery	Nouveau Zinfandel	Sémillon
Villa Armando	Vino Rustico	
Wente Bros.	Pinot Noir	Blanc de Blancs

SOUTH BAY

Grapes

WINERIES	REDS	WHITES
Almadén Vineyards	Grenache Rose	Pinot Noir
Bargetto Santa Cruz Winery	Barbera	Chenin Blanc
Gemello Winery	Zinfandel	Chardonnay
Mirassou Vineyards	Cabernet Sauvignon	Chenin Blanc
Paul Masson	Rubion	Emerald Riesling
Novitiate of Los Gatos	Black Muscat	
Pedrizetti	Barbera, Petite Sirah	
Rapazzini	Zinfandel, Petite Sirah	
Ridge	Cabernet Sauvignon, Zinfandel	
San Martin	Zinfandel	Johannisberg Riesling

MONTEREY AND SANTA BARBARA

Grapes

Monterey

WINERIES	REDS	WHITES
Chalone	Pinot Noir	Pinot Blanc
Monterey Peninsula Winery	Zinfandel	Riesling
The Monterey Vineyard	Zinfandel	Del Mar Ranch
Turgeon & Lohr	Cabernet Sauvignon	Chardonnay

Santa Barbara

The Firestone Vineyard	Pinot Noir	Gewürztraminer
Hoffman Mountain Ranch	Pinot Noir	Sylvaner
Tepusquet Cellars	Cabernet Sauvignon	White Riesling

BOUTIQUE WINERIES OF CALIFORNIA

There are dozens of small wineries in California producing exceptional wines in limited quantity and with limited distribution and are called boutique wineries. (Such wines can often be ordered through your local wine shop.) Many of the wineries maintain mailing lists and wines can be bought direct where state laws permit.

Napa

Cakebread Cellars, Rutherford
Carneros Creek Winery, Napa
Caymus Vineyards, St. Helena
Chateau Chevalier, St. Helena
Diamond Creek Vineyards, Calistoga
Mayacamas Vineyards, Napa
Mount Veeder Winery, Napa

Nichelini Vineyards, St. Helena
Pope Valley Winery, St. Helena
Raymond Vineyards, St. Helena
Rutherford Hill, Rutherford
Stag's Leap Winery, Yountville
Stonegate Winery, Calistoga
Trefethen Vineyards, Napa
Veedercrest Vineyards, Emeryville
Villa Mount Eden, Oakville
Yverdon Vineyards, St. Helena

Sonoma

Alexander Valley Vineyards, Healdsburg
Edmeades Vineyards, Philo
Gundlach-Bundschu Wine Company, Vineburg
Hacienda Wine Cellars, Sonoma
Hanzell Vineyards, Sonoma
Hop Kiln Winery, Healdsburg
Johnson's of Alexander Valley, Healdsburg
Landmark Vineyards, Windsor
Mill Creek Vineyards, Healdsburg
Russian River Vineyards, Forestville
Sotoyome Winery, Healdsburg
Vina Vista Vineyards, Geyserville

South of San Francisco

David Bruce Winery, Los Gatos
Durney Vineyard, Carmel Valley
Enz Vineyards, Hollister
Estrella River Vineyards, Paso Robles

Live Oaks Winery, Gilroy
Llords & Elwood Winery, Beverly Hills
Los Alamos Winery, Los Alamos
York Mountain Winery, Templeton
Zaca Mesa Winery, Los Olivos

Note: Several large vineyards have been planted, but their wines will not be available until well into the 1980s. Wines from the smallest wineries, producing less than two thousand cases, are generally sold to visitors and friends.

Wineries of New York and Elsewhere

THE NORTHWEST, NEW YORK, AND ELSEWHERE

Vineyards once flourished from the Hudson to the Mississippi, but most of them succumbed to the Concord, a grape for jelly and juice that is still used to make ordinary sweet wines. A few native grapes remained to make odd wines with a musky character described as foxy—mostly Catawbas and Delawares and Niagaras around Lake Erie and Scuppernongs in the south. By mid-century these native grapes had been successfully crossed with European *vinifera* to produce French-American hybrids that are now replacing the old vines. There has been some success with Chardonnay and Johannisberg Riesling, but except for a few wines of the Northwest and New York, most bottlings are drunk locally. Wines are made in every state and some will get to distant markets in the 1980s.

The Northwest

With more daylight during the growing season and a somewhat more rigorous climate than California, Washington and Oregon provide an environment more like Europe for the *vinifera* grapes. The wines are proving to be remarkable, and while there are a score of vineyards, only the wines of Ste. Michelle reach major markets.

Grapes

WINERY	REDS	WHITES
Ste. Michelle	Cabernet Sauvignon	Johannisberg Riesling
	Pinot Noir	Gewürztraminer
	Grenache Rosé	Sémillon

New York

The Finger Lakes region in the center of the state produces most of the wines found in major markets. Largest of the wineries is Taylor Wine Company, producing a full line of blends, their Great Western division offering a line of premium wines. Along the Hudson, several small wineries send a few bottles to New York City, while some more come from Chatauqua County, bordering Lake Erie.

	Grapes	
WINERIES	REDS	WHITES
Hudson Valley & Long Island		
Benmarl Vineyards	Chancellor	Seyval Blanc
Hargrave Vineyards	Pinot Noir	Chardonnay
The Finger Lakes		
Bully Hill Wine Company	Bully Hill Red	Seyval Blanc
Great Western (Pleasant Valley Wine Company)	Chelois, Baco Noir	
Gold Seal	Charles Fournier Blanc de Blancs	
Taylor Wine Company	Lake Country Red	Lake Country white
Vinifera Wine Cellars		Johannisberg Riesling Chardonnay
Widmer's Wine Cellars	Pinot Noir	Delaware
Chatauqua		
Johnson Estate Winery	Dry Red	Seyval Blanc

Pennsylvania and Ohio

Vineyards stretch all along Lake Erie's southern shore, extending beyond Cleveland, with a cluster on the Pennsylvania border around the town of North East, whose wines occasionally reach the cities. The Niagara Peninsula of Ontario is the northern shore and there Inniskillen, Bright's, Charal, Jordan, and Château Gai provide Toronto with good wines from Chardonnay, de Chaunac, and other hybrids, rarely exported. A dozen small vineyards in eastern Pennsylvania and to the west along the Ohio River produce wines for local markets.

	Grapes	
WINERIES	REDS	WHITES
Pennsylvania		
Mazza Vineyards		Traminer
Penn Shore Winery	Ruby Cascade	
Presque Isle Wine Cellars	Chambourcin	
Ohio		
Cedar Hill Wine Company	Millot-Chambourcin Red	Riesling and
Markko Vineyards		Chardonnay

Note: Many small wineries with experimental plots of *vinifera* and hybrid grapes have been established in the mid-Atlantic and the midwestern states, notably Boordy Vineyards in Maryland; Tabor Hill Wine Cellars, Bronte Winery and Leelanau Wine Cellars in Michigan; and Wiederkehr Wine Cellars in Arkansas. Their wines are worth trying out of curiosity, as are those from the many small experimental and hobby vineyards.

Fortified Wines:
Sherry and Port (Porto)

SHERRY

A complex storing system makes sherry what it is. Young wines are fermented in small casks, then poured into the top row of a three-tiered system of barrels called the cradle, or *criadera*. Wines are drawn off the oldest tier, which is refilled from the one above, which is refilled from the newest wines. Less than half the wine is drawn off in any one year. The wine stays at least a year in each of the tiers and then goes into a similar system called the *solera,* or foundation. The age stops in a *solera* may be five years, or even longer.

The newly fermented wine may develop a film on top called the *flor,* or "flower." These wines are destined to become Finos. Barrels with nutty tastes become Amontillados, those with a great amount of smell become Olorosos. Each goes into a *solera* of its own type, the young wines taking on the character of the older wines as they pass through the tiers. For shipment, wines from several *soleras* are blended to the style the firm has established for its customers. For Cream Sherries, sweetening wines similarly aged are blended with Olorosos. Some *soleras* are a century old, bottles from them containing a fraction of the oldest wine.

PORTO

The great wine of Portugal has been so much imitated that the name of the only great red fortified wine has been named for the town from which it is shipped. All genuine Port is now Porto—even though the town is Oporto and the wines are aged across the river in Vila Nova da Gaia.

The rarest of all are Vintage Portos, which are allowed to age for decades before being drunk, three of them being considered about minimum. Vintages to lay down for your children include 1975, 1973, 1970, 1967, 1966, 1963, and 1960. You might begin tasting, to see how they are coming along, vintages of 1958, 1955, 1950, 1948, 1945, and 1942. Vintages of 1934 and 1935 are fine, but the greatest one occasionally available is 1927. Taste when you can the 1912, the 1908, 1896, or 1878.

Late-bottled Vintage Porto, drawn from barrels after four years, develops much more quickly than Vintage Porto, which is bottled after two years. These wines throw heavy sediments—it is called the crust—and the wines must be decanted before serving. Portos quickly lose their fruity brilliance, once opened, so it is customary to finish the bottle at a sitting. Many a grand old English gentleman of the last century used to be able to drink his decanter of Porto alone, and certainly with a friend, but a party of four or six is perhaps necessary today to do justice to a fine vintage, or even a Tawny or a still-younger Ruby.

Classic Wine=Food Affinities

Some combinations are unsurpassed—Champagne and caviar, Chablis with oysters, Meursault with salmon, Bordeaux with lamb, Burgundy with pheasant, Sauternes with pears and Brie, Port with walnuts. There are many more—wider choices and still narrower ones—some where various foods complement a single wine.

What goes well with dry Sherry, for instance? The Spanish like to serve *tapas* (bits of food), for instance, in the middle of the morning or the middle of the afternoon, with glasses of Fino, chilled. Almonds, fresh or salted filberts, even peanuts in or out of the shell. Olives, green or ripe. Slivers of ham, bits of sausage, broiled liver or kidneys on skewers, even cubes of cheese on toothpicks. Also boiled shrimp served cold, with or without mayonnaise.

Shrimp is really better with Manzanilla, the Fino matured on the seacoast that seems to have a special salty tang. So do other bits of fish or seafood, or shellfish, served hot or cold, pickled or dressed with oil and vinegar. Montilla, the unfortified wine like dry Sherry, is good with all these things, but especially with air-dried Serrano ham, olives stuffed with almonds, broiled garlic sausages, hot cheese sticks.

But hot cheese sticks are best with Champagne, which is also served with slivers of ham. Champagne is absolutely marvelous with pâtés that contain chicken or ham, with canapés (canapés seem to have been invented for Champagne), with *foie gras.*

You can see what happens. Taste memories rove. Start with things that complement a wine, then similar wines that go with the various foods. These widen the range of tastes. Then there are the contrasting tastes—Fino with plain shrimp quite different from Fino with shrimp and mayonnaise or Fino with shrimp vinaigrette. These various combinations mark the joys of wine, the theater of tastes.

The suggestions below follow the classic patterns, a chart not detailed, but to be particularized by the explorers.

APPETIZERS	*Any chilled wine, still or sparkling:*
Hors d'Oeuvre Pâté, spreads, dips Smoked salmon, ham	dry Fino or Manzanilla Sherries, all dry whites, any rosés, and light reds like Beaujolais
Canapés	Champagne
Caviar	Champagne

SHELLFISH	*White wines, Champagnes, sparkling wines:*
Clams, mussels	Blanc de Blancs, Graves, Chenin Blanc
Oysters	Chablis, Muscadet, Chardonnay, Pinot Blanc, Champagne
Scallops, crab	Sauvignon Blanc or Fumé Blanc, Sancerre, Sylvaner, Johannisberg Riesling, Soave
Lobster	Gewürztraminer, Pinot Gris, Sauternes

FISH	*White wines, Fino or Manzanilla Sherries:*
Pan-fried	Light, dry whites—Graves, Loire, Alsace, Chenin Blanc, Sémillon, Soave
Poached, grilled	Meursault, Chardonnay, Moselle
With sauces	White Burgundy, Loire, Sauvignon Blanc
Salmon, tuna	Meursault, Corton, Montrachet, Chardonnay
Fish stews	Full whites, rosés

FOWL	*Full whites, rosés, light reds:*
Chicken or turkey	Chardonnay, Meursault, Graves, rosé Beaujolais, Médoc, Saint-Emilion, Cabernet
Game birds	Côte-de-Beaune reds, Gamay, Pinot Noir

SMOKED OR SPICED MEATS	*Full whites, rosés, light reds:*
Ham, pork, sausages	Rhine or Alsatian wines, Sauvignon Blanc or Fumé Blanc, Chenin Blanc, Johannisberg Riesling, Sylvaner, Pinot Gris

MEATS	*Red wines or rosés:*
Veal, sweetbreads	Beaujolais or Côte-de-Beaune reds, Pinot Noir, Cabernet Sauvignon, Chianti.
Lamb	Graves, Médoc, Saint-Emilion, Pomerol, Cabernet Sauvignon, Merlot, Rioja
Beef	Burgundy, Saint-Emilion, Pinot Noir, Gamay Beaujolais, Barolo, Valtellina, Rioja
Stews, pot roasts	Beaujolais, Côtes-du-Rhône, Valpolicella, Zinfandel, Petite Sirah
Game—venison, wild duck, rabbit	Burgundies, Zinfandel, Petite Sirah, Hermitage, Côte Rotie, Barolo, Barbaresco

CHEESE   *Any dry wine: red, white, rosé:*

DESSERT   *Sweet wines:* Sauternes, *Spätlese,* or
                  Auslese, Tokay, Johannisberg Riesling.

Nuts, fruit   Port, Madeira, Cream Sherry

FOODS FOR GREAT WINES

Great wines possess subtleties that often go unnoticed when the foods are pronounced in flavor. The custom is to serve a great wine after a younger, lesser one, late in the meal or with a separate cheese course, although the wine may not get the consideration it warrants in the general conviviality of the meal. Today, a great wine is often served by itself, before a meal, so that attention can be brought to bear. With our simpler meals of fewer courses, many like to serve a great wine with a main course suited to it, then switch to an entirely different wine that may be younger or lighter, with cheese or dessert. The necessity is to suit the wine to the guests, not to serve great wines when attention is directed to other matters. Listed here are foods that enhance great wines, and the temperatures at which the wines are best served.

WHITE WINES	TEMPERA-TURE*	FOOD
Fine or Amontillado Sherry	Cold	Salted almonds, filberts, prosciutto
Champagne, sparkling wines	Iced	Caviar, cold dishes

Rhine *Kabinett* or Johannisberg Riesling	Cold	Simple fish or chicken dishes, ham
Rhine or Moselle, *Spätlese* or *Auslese*	Cold	Before or after meals, with a sweet or cheese soufflé, light pastry, pears or apples
Graves, Sancerre, Sauvignon Blanc, Sémillon	Cold	Fish, veal, or chicken dishes with light sauces
Chablis, Great or First Growths; Chardonnay	Cold	Oysters, cold fowl, veal, ham, shellfish
Corton, Montrachet, Meursault, Great and First Growths	Cold	Poached salmon, lobster, special veal or fish dishes

RED WINES

Beaune, Volnay, First Growths	Cool	Roast beef, veal, chicken, pheasant
Burgundy, Great Growths	Cool	Special beef dishes, wild fowl, cheese
Rhônes: Hermitage, Côte Rotie	Cool	Beef, game, wild fowl, cheese
Bordeaux Classed Growths: Médoc, Graves, Pomerol	Cool	Leg or rack of lamb, roast fowl, cheese

Saint-Emilion, Rioja Reserva, Cabernet Sauvignon, Barolo	Cool	Steak, beef roast, or filet, wild fowl, cheese

Temperature ranges:

Cool is what was once called room temperature, between 60°F.–70°F.

Cold: 50°F.–55°F.

Iced: below 50°F, 10 to 15 minutes in an ice bucket, or 30 to 40 minutes on lowest shelf of refrigerator.

Index